The Charm of CHARLESTON

ARCHITECTURE, CULTURE, AND NATURE

Stories of The South Carolina Lowcountry

WRITTEN BY MICHAEL TROUCHE

Michael Trouche is a seventh-generation Charlestonian whose interest in the city's history has been a life-long passion. The Trouche family has been an integral part of Charleston since 1792, recognized by the Gibbes Museum of Art, the Charleston Musuem, and official U.S. military records for contributions and service to the city.

Michael's acclaimed "Carolina Camera" and "Carolina Explorer" television series provided audiences with more than twenty years of entertaining and educational programming devoted to local culture, nature and adventure, for which he has won numerous state, regional and national awards. Michael is also a licensed Charleston tour guide and tourism events speaker, and has written extensively for local publications, performed in area theater groups, as well as teaching at both college and high school levels.

Published by
Charleston Postcard Co., Inc.
182 Plymouth Avenue, Charleston, SC 29412
Phone: 843-762-6100   Fax: 843-762-5711
charlestonpostcard@comcast.net

©2008
2nd Edition

Photography: Joe McLemore, David Reese,
Buddy Moffet, Bryan Riggs.
Design: Alan Dubrovo

Special acknowledgements:

Sweetgrass: page 10 - basket by Vera Manigault, photographed courtesy of Michael Allen, Education Specialist, National Park Service.

Fort Sumter & Why the Palmetto State: Richard W. Hatcher III, Historian - Fort Sumter National Monument and Charles Pinckney National Historic Site.

Man of Iron: Rossie Colter, Public Administrator for Philip Simmons.
For more information about Philip Simmons and the Foundation, contact:
Philip Simmons Foundation, Inc., P.O.Box 21585, Charleston, SC 29413-1585
Tel: 843-571-6445 or fax: 843-571-6435 · www.philipsimmons.org

Getting to Know Charleston's Bottom: Artifacts and fossils from the private collection of John Taylor, sales@sharksteeth.com.

Reef photos - compliments of South Carolina Department of Natural Resources.

Designed in the U.S.A.
Printed in China
©OKI, Inc. 2008
BK-CH-03

HARLESTON IS A CITY AND AN EXPERIENCE LIKE NO OTHER IN AMERICA.

Blessed with a unique combination of historic splendor, cultural charm and natural beauty, the "Holy City" is a pleasurable destination to visit and a wonderful place to call home. With its waterfront vistas and stunning architecture, its unforgettable aromas of sweetgrass and magnolia, and its singular sounds of colonial church bells and horse carriages, Charleston is as sensually overwhelming as it is a timeless treasure.

The purpose of this book is to enhance the enjoyment and appreciation of Charleston with a lively insider's look at the exceptional places, people and events that make the city so special. That incredible allure of history, mystery, and enchantment is truly the essence of the delightful city we know as Charleston.

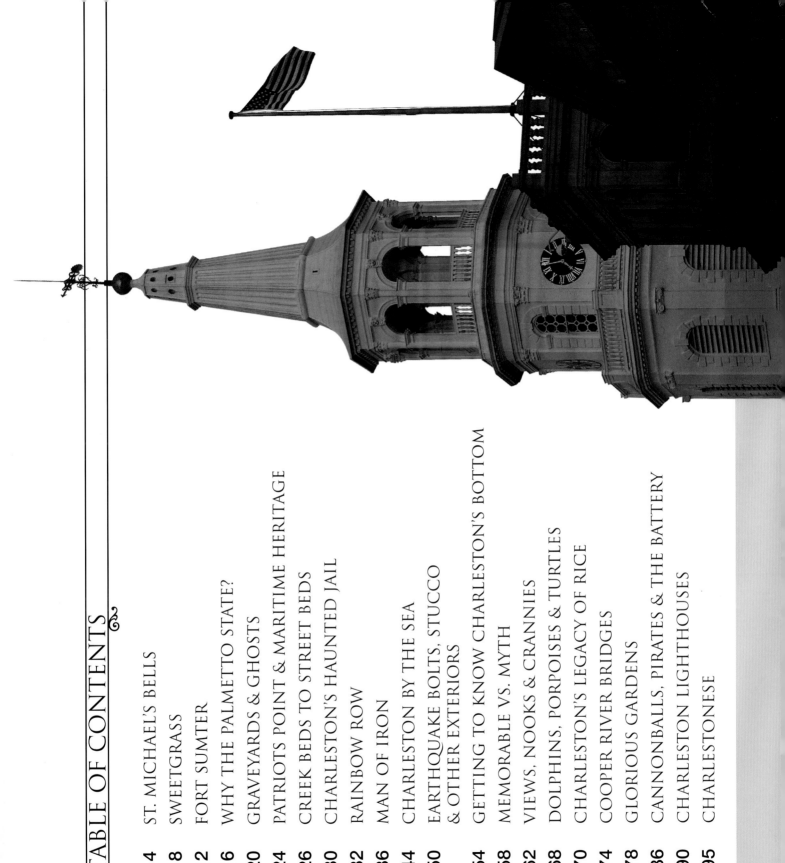

TABLE OF CONTENTS

ST. MICHAEL'S BELLS

Proof that Charleston charm runs rings around most other places in America is repeated at least every fifteen minutes along the town's historic skyline, as bell towers of various denominations echo a centuries-old reminder as to why it's called the "Holy City".

Charleston's oldest and most storied steeple is the 186-foot belfry tower atop St. Michael's Episcopal Church on the corner of Broad and Meeting Streets, where it has stood soundly against the worst onslaughts that nature and mankind could muster since 1761. Inside the steeple, a set of eight massive bronze bells are the second oldest in North America, having endured their own incredible set of circumstances to hang on to that position. The fact that each bell is named for an angel or archangel may have helped protect them through fire, earthquakes, hurricanes, tornadoes, cannonballs and seven trans-Atlantic crossings to keep their inspirational tone intact.

This high-altitude octave, whose largest bell weighs in at 1945 pounds, was cast at the Lester and Pack Foundry in England, imported to Charleston, and rung for the first time in 1764. Balanced in a belfry frame between wheels that allow them to swing 360 degrees, the bells were precision-tuned to sound a scale of notes ranging from a high tenor to a low treble. Controlled by hand from ropes that dangle into a steeple ringing room below, the bells were originally designed to be rung by pulling the ropes in sequence, creating a harmonious peal known as "change-ringing".

St. Michael's has offered up much more than prayer since colonial times, however, as its lofty perch overlooking the old city created sight and sound advantages that were used for secular purposes as well. For example, the steeple bells served as the city's official fire alarm until the 1880's. A "steepleman" was stationed in the tower, and in the event of a fire, would toll the largest bell, then step out on the steeple balcony and point a lantern attached to the end of a pole in the direction of the blaze, showing the way to fire brigades below. The tower was also used as a military observation post for Charleston's defenses in numerous wars over the years, and many sharp-eyed soldiers were ordered up the narrow steps of the old steeple to ring out warnings of impending attacks.

Opposite: View of St. Michael's at Dusk

View from St. Michael's Steeple

Unfortunately, history has also sounded some sour notes for the bells, which were removed by the city's British captors during the Revolution and taken back to England in 1782. Returned to Charleston after the war and restored inside the tower, the bells once again went into military service during the War of 1812 and later during the War between the States,

The Bell Tower

when Union gunners in the blockading fleet lobbed so many shells at St. Michael's that the steeple was painted black to make a less-inviting target. Unlike many other Charleston church bells that were donated to the Confederate cause to be melted down into cannon, those in St. Michael's were shipped to Columbia, S.C., for safe-keeping - or so it was believed.

Ironically, General Sherman mettled with the church's precious metal by burning the warehouses in which the bells were stored, cracking the outer surfaces. After considerable hand-wringing, the damaged bells were shipped back to England again for recasting and were lifted back into St. Michael's in 1867. Yet it wasn't long before another familiar tune played havoc with St. Michael's as the church took direct hits from Charleston's great cyclone of 1885, the great earthquake of 1886, the great tornado of 1938 (on St. Michael's day, naturally), and the not-so-great Hurricane Hugo in 1989. This unsettling interim sank the steeple a full eight feet, knocked it off plumb temporarily, and left the belfry frame too crooked to conduct proper change-ringing.

With St. Michael's most recent restoration in 1993, the bells were sent to England's Whitechapel Foundry once more for re-tuning, the belfry frame was rebuilt, and the sounds of change-ringing firmly reestablished. Today, peals are rung at St. Michael's for Sunday services, weddings, funerals and special events, such as Carolina Day, June 28, celebrating Charleston's 1776 victory over the British, a special irony considering the origins of the instruments. The eight bells perform an octave - tenor E-flat, F, G, A-flat, B-flat, C, D and treble E-flat - rung in varying patterns known as "rounds" by individual ringers pulling the ends of bell ropes, called "sallies". Even though hundreds of pounds of momentum on the other end of each rope could yank pullers through the ceiling, change-ringing is more skill than brute force, as orderly timing in strict mathematical beats and sequences maintains clarity in an acoustical sensation now regularly offered by more churches in the Charleston area than any other city on the continent.

St. Michael's Steeple

Other historic churches around Charleston that have renovated their bell towers for change-ringing include The Cathedral Church of St. Luke and St. Paul, Grace Episcopal Church, and Stella Maris Roman Catholic Church, all influenced by the resonating success of the St. Michael's ringers. In fact, Msgr. Lawrence McInerny, pastor of Stella Maris, learned the ropes of change- ringing by practicing in the ringing room at St. Michael's until, rumor has it, the Pope pulled some strings and got Protestant foundries in England to cast bells for Catholics as well.

As in many Charleston churches, the bells of St. Michael's are also electronically timed to chime in synchronization with the steeple clock in fifteen minute intervals on a daily basis, and many residents set their watches to the familiar refrain. With the background of catastrophes and cannonballs that have targeted Charleston's oldest church, it's understandable that St. Michael's punctuality may occasionally be off by a stroke or two, but the tune of the old bells is as unmistakable and vibrant as ever.

St. Michael's Bells are the second oldest in America

The Ringing Room

SWEETGRASS

Each day on sidewalks and along roadways around Charleston, one of America's oldest cultural traditions is begun from scratch all over again in the form of hand-woven sweetgrass baskets. More than a quaint folk-art, the sweetgrass basket is an enduring symbol of people's ability to make the most of hardships in life. Weaving skill has been passed down, generation to generation, for more than three centuries among descendants of African slaves, who turned nature's simplicity into lasting function and beauty.

Sweetgrass gets its name from a pungent chemical in the smooth, slender leaves that, when dried, gives the plant a pleasing smell similar to fresh cut grass or bales of hay. Found in wetland bottoms along the coast, this sturdy, supple perennial sprouts leaves two feet long or more, which are harvested by hand into sheafs that must be completely dried before weaving. Most gatherers spread sweetgrass on the ground in thin sheets to dry, but because wind can easily scatter leaves, others prefer heaving bundles on the sloping roof tops of their houses to block wind and get more direct sunlight.

Methods of converting sweetgrass into baskets are creative and diverse as well, and will usually include additions of bull rush, long leaf pine, and strips of palmetto fronds, known in Gullah tradition as "fan o'metta".

Baskets are woven by taking the root ends of the sweetgrass or "heads", and tying them into knots, before twisting and wrapping with stitches made from the other binding materials. As more leaves are fed into the weave, baskets begin to take shape in the form of tight coils, wound seamlessly, row by row, in outwardly-radiating spirals.

Creating space for each stitch to pass through the ever-increasing coils, weavers use one, basic tool, the "nail bone". Generations ago, this would have been an animal bone, typically from a pig or cow, and occasionally,

Basketmaker with weaving tool known as a Nail Bone

weavers from the past used nails or pieces of glass. In recent times, the preferred stitch-maker has been a metal spoon or fork broken off at the handle tip and sharpened to a point, as weavers near St. Michael's Church, the old city market or at stands on Highway 17 in Mount Pleasant work wonders with the sawed-off piece of cutlery. And although the weaver's tool may be shiny and silver, it is still known as the nail bone.

Originally, sweetgrass weaving was a labor of necessity, as slave families had to make their own implements for work as well as for personal use. The domestic baskets were usually woven bowl-shaped or with handles for carrying food, clothes or other belongings. For work, broad "fannin" baskets were woven flat for the primary plantation task of separating rice kernels from chaff.

From the bare essentials found on the ground around old plantations, came the development of useful tools, housewares and a form of artful expression that helped cope with the drudgery of slavery existence, and today sweetgrass has a cultural tie as strong as the tight weaves that have lasted for generations. One rare, but time-honored technique is the "family basket", an ongoing sweetgrass project purposely continued as a work

Sweetgrass

Sweetgrass Baskets

break off just above the roots, leaving enough to grow back. But doing so puts bare hands very close to ground where cottonmouth moccasins are known to lurk. Adding to the misery is the fact that sweetgrass areas are typically breeding grounds for mosquitoes, ticks and redbugs, and weavers can easily feel the pain of creation before they've begun.

What might seem to the passing tourist as somewhat expensive - big baskets can fetch $250 or more - the finished sweetgrass is always a bargain when broken down to an hourly wage, and any one who has watched the painstaking pace of a sidewalk basket being created has also been entertained at the weaver's expense. It's okay to trot out those bartering skills, but don't expect to make much headway, and don't expect a receipt or a product guarantee, although most weavers do take Visa.

What is carried back to other parts of America and placed on shelves, hung on walls, or used as a base for flower arrangements is a tribute to the creativity, durability and longevity of the sweetgrass people and their art form, which, like the plant itself, has lingering roots. After all, one old saying among weavers was that you may not live long enough to finish a sweetgrass basket, but a finished basket may surely outlive you.

in progress so that succeeding generations of weavers can have a part in the same creation as their ancestors.

Most sweetgrass woven these days deviates from historic tradition, however, as today's baskets are typically more ornamental and usually for sale to someone else. Creative form is now valued more than practical use in what has become a thriving cottage industry. Exceptional skill and imagination are displayed in weaves that feature hinges, braids, arches, domes, and latches. Basket shapes can be flared, or "played out", as well as closed, or "hauled in". A "right-handed" basket is one that coils clockwise, while a "left-handed" basket runs counter-clockwise. Intricacies of design include color variations from differing percentages of materials used. Long leaf pine, for example adds a russet hue, while bull rush turns tawny when completely dry, and stitched in fluctuating thickness in the form of diamonds, loops, and rings, often seems more sculpted than tied by hand.

The term "basket" cannot adequately describe much of the handiwork conceived and achieved in sweetgrass, and during Charleston's Moja Arts Festival, which celebrates African contributions to the city's culture, annual prizes are awarded to the most artistic weaving concepts.

Sweetgrass

Sweetgrass can be stored in dry areas out of sunlight for years without loss of flexibility or strength, and many a weaver has taken up where he or she left off months, or even years ago. Just as time has proven the durability of sweetgrass baskets and enhanced their cultural status, time is the most unavoidable element in a process that is by no means a soft touch. There's no mass production, and even the smallest and simplest finished shapes will take many long hours of methodical stitching, tying and wrapping - and that's assuming all materials are readily available.

Not only are large expanses of wild sweetgrass becoming more rare, the actual work in gathering has always had inherent hazards. Growing thigh-high in thick clumps on low-lying wetlands and barrier islands, sweetgrass is natural cover for snakes and other biting things you don't want to reach into blindly. Harvesting is done by twisting the long, thin leaves until they

Opposite: Sweetgrass Fanning Basket

FORT SUMTER

For thousands who visit Charleston each year, the local name seemingly most recognized is Fort Sumter, and even those tourists who are only vaguely familiar with details of our history are intrigued by the chance to explore this famous site. Internationally- renowned for its role in the explosive beginning of the American Civil War, Fort Sumter's allure is enhanced by its unique location atop a sandy shoal at the entrance to Charleston Harbor. Easily seen from numerous promenades along the city's waterfront, the great old fort that stood so defiantly against attacks from land and sea is now an enticing and accommodating destination.

Construction of Fort Sumter was begun in 1829 to help strengthen U.S. coastal defenses, the unusual location chosen for its dominating position next to ship channels entering the harbor. Initially, 70,000 tons of granite and rock were brought in by ship from as far away as New England to create a solid foundation on two and a half acres of bottom almost completely submerged at high tide. Although brick was the primary building material, another construction method was tabby, a mixture of mortar and oyster shell.

Fort Sumter's pentagon design featured three tiers of guns on walls that reached fifty feet above the low tide mark, providing a potentially deadly concentration of firepower against likely naval attack from any side. Fort Sumter is named for Revolutionary War hero General Thomas Sumter, the "Carolina Gamecock" whose relentless efforts against the British helped turn the tide in America's favor. Ironically, the turning tide of America's political landscape in 1860 would make the Sumter name even more noteworthy.

The fort was still under construction when South Carolina seceded from the Union on December 20, 1860, and the Federal garrison at nearby Fort Moultrie occupied Fort Sumter six days later. Anyone who's taken American History knows what happened next, as Confederates fired on the fort on April 12, 1861, to initiate the War Between the States. Surrounded by Confederate gunners who ringed the harbor with considerable firepower, Fort Sumter's first action was to be subjected to

more than 30 hours of continuous bombardment, including incendiary "hotshot" that set much of the fort on fire. Nearly overcome by heat and smoke, the Union garrison bravely returned fire, earning the admiration of Confederates who actually cheered rounds fired from the fort. Ironically, Fort Sumter's first fatal casualty occurred after the fort was surrendered to the Confederates, when a Union soldier was killed firing a departing salute to the American flag.

Flags at Fort Sumter National Monument

Although most of the substantial military action at Fort Sumter took place in the four years that followed, history treats the fort's remaining service with general obscurity. Garrisoned by Confederates from 1861 to 1865, Fort Sumter would continue to be a remarkable symbol of courage and determination as well as representing passage into the era of modern warfare. The fort was considered the key to Charleston's defenses during the Civil War, and was pounded from sea and nearby Morris Island as invading Union forces with newly-invented ironclads and rifled cannon gradually reduced the brick structure to rubble.

On April 7, 1863, a squadron of nine ironclads, featuring some of the most powerful ships in the world, was sent to overwhelm the apparently

outdated and steam past it to capture Charleston. But Confederate gunners responded with more than two thousand shots in the space of two and a half hours, sinking one ironclad and inflicting enough damage on the remaining ships that the attack was called off. Despite 15-inch guns, iron plating, and mobility, naval attack would not succeed against Fort Sumter, and the Federal tactics changed.

Interior of Fort Sumter National Monument

Beginning in August 1863, Fort Sumter became the focus of one of the longest sieges in military history - 587 consecutive days. During that period, there were three stages of intense shelling over a period of 117 days, combined with eight minor bombardments over the course of 40 days, as well as another 280 days of intermittent shelling, for a total of 437 days that the fort was under Federal fire. By that stage of the war, bigger and more effective cannon could fire projectiles weighing hundreds of pounds accurately from miles away, and dairies from defenders inside mention that even rats had trouble finding any cover.

During a 41-day stretch in which 18,677 shells were fired into the fort, observers described it as a "volcanic pile" in which only a handful of cannons remained serviceable. Constant fires were fought by filling gaps in walls with cotton bales soaked in wet sand and salt water, and defenders' best protection was to dig tunnels through the ever-increasing debris.

For the last 18 months of Confederate occupation, the only cannon fired from Fort Sumter was a mountain howitzer, as the small garrison was converted to an infantry outpost whose resistance was primarily in the form of rifle shots aimed at Yankee gunners on Morris Island. One Union attempt to storm the walls of Fort Sumter in September, 1863, in a night-time amphibious assault was met with fierce resistance by the city's Charleston Battalion, whose volleys included heaving pieces of rubble at the attackers, earning them the nickname "the brickbat battalion".

Another creative attempt to finish Fort Sumter was made in August, 1864, by floating rafts filled with gunpowder and timed fuses to explode against the fort's walls, but shifting tides foiled the plan, creating merely a noisy diversion.

Despite being hit by 3500 tons of metal, and suffering through constant attack and fires, Fort Sumter never surrendered, but did outlast several Federal guns that burst after firing so many rounds at the fort. When Rear Admiral John Dahlgren of the attacking squadron demanded that Fort Sumter surrender during the siege, the Confederate reply was, "Inform Admiral Dahlgren that he may have Fort Sumter when he can take it and hold it." He never did.

Supported by big guns from surrounding Confederate batteries on Sullivan's and James Islands, Fort Sumter's defenses helped keep Charleston from being taken until the city was evacuated in February, 1865.

Interior of Fort Sumter National Monument

100 pound parrott gun

Tour boats bring crowds each day to Fort Sumter, now manned by National Park Service rangers who give history talks or simply encourage folks to wander the grounds. The thirty-minute ride back and forth shows off the beauty of Charleston harbor, lined with graceful houses and church steeples, and filled with sailboats, incoming container ships, diving pelicans and splashing dolphins. It's difficult, amid the pleasant surroundings, to imagine the horrors of war, and even with its artillery, artifacts, and pock-marked walls, Fort Sumter is a peaceful reminder of the price freedom often brings.

The effects of the bombardment reduced Fort Sumter to its present one-story level, and holes are still visible in the fort walls. Repaired after the war, the fort was primarily used as an unmanned lighthouse station until the Spanish-American War, and in 1898, massive concrete Battery Isaac Huger was built on what was the original fort's parade ground. Equipped with big seacoast and anti-submarine guns during World Wars I and II, Fort Sumter's garrison fired hundreds of training rounds well into the 20th century, but the last angry shot came from the fort during the 1860's.

Fort Sumter's role as a military installation ended after World War II when the U.S. Army closed the fort, but it soon reclaimed its significant role when transferred to the National Park Service as a national monument in 1948.

Today, Battery Isaac Huger houses a well-designed fort museum with a wealth of original artifacts and descriptive displays and pictures from Fort Sumter's distinguished history. But outside on the ramparts and

View of Fort Sumter National Monument from Charleston Harbor

in remaining original gun embrasures are the most memorable sites of Fort Sumter. Still high over incoming sea lanes, and with a commanding view of Charleston harbor, the city skyline and surrounding islands, the windswept guns and flags stir an undeniable admiration for those on both sides who held their ground there, and it is truly awe-inspiring to stand on this small island fort and watch from the same perspective from which other eyes looked as the concentrated force of America's most emotional epoch focused upon them.

WHY THE PALMETTO STATE?

he tree on South Carolina's state flag makes it easy to remember that this is the "Palmetto State" and easy to forget that we were once known as the "Iodine State".

The latter was printed on state license plates from 1930 to 1934 to promote the medicinal qualities of iodine found in South Carolina's soil, but, thankfully, the coming of iodized salt saved us from a truly distasteful nickname. Today, South Carolina license plates display the palmetto tree, a much more recognizable symbol than iodine, and one that can be found on everything from to surfboards to underwear.

In truth, the palmetto is much more common to Florida, where it is also the state tree, but it only took a relatively small number of our own variety to make a lasting impact back in 1776.

In March of that year, the province of South Carolina had formally revolted from English rule, and preparations were made for the naval attack that was sure to come from the powerful British fleet. The target would certainly be the colonial capitol then known as Charlestown, whose access from the sea required ships to sail close to nearby Sullivan's Island into the harbor.

On this sandy barrier island, the newly-organized 2nd South Carolina regiment was sent under the command of Colonel William Moultrie to help finish construction of a fort being built to defend the city. Consisting of the most readily available materials - island palmetto trees and soil - what became known as "Fort Sullivan" took shape by packing earth and sand between stacks of horizontal bundles of logs, and building enclosed artillery platforms that stood twenty feet high. These in turn were protected by a 16-foot thick earthwork parapet stretching nearly two hundred yards long.

Only the one side of the fort facing the sea was completed when British ships arrived off the coast in early June, and only thirty-one guns were ready for action when the fleet began its attack on the morning of June 28, 1776.

When observing the American defenders dug in behind hastily-built piles of palmetto logs, the British commander, Sir Peter Parker, offered up an ironic insult by scoffing at the group of southerners as "cowardly Yankees". With his powerful fleet packing the awesome firepower of 270 guns, Parker then commenced what he thought would be a swift and thorough shellacking of the enemy.

Defense of Fort Sullivan, SC. courtesy of Fort Sumter National Monument

The battle was one-sided, but it was the "Yankees" who won, as withering fire caused one English frigate to run aground, where it was abandoned and burned, while seriously damaging five more. A British naval officer later described how incoming rounds seemed to have no effect on the palmetto log defenses, writing that "not a single shell could do any mischief". The return fire did plenty of mischief, however, and legend says that Sir Peter, whose flagship Bristol was badly damaged, suffered the ultimate indignity of having his pants blown off.

What turned the tide was what the palmetto had inside - a fibrous, stringy core that smothered the British cannonballs. Fire-resistant and not inclined to fracture into splinters, the palmetto facade was impervious to the kind of collateral damage that ship broadsides had on other wooden or brick defenses, and with the spongy logs absorbing most British salvos, the

Aerial view of Fort Moultrie

Gorget

South Carolinians only lost a total of twelve killed and 25 wounded. Charlestown was saved, and a week after the battle, the Declaration of Independence was signed and a new nation was begun.

Renamed Fort Moultrie after the battle in honor of its commander, the fort was damaged by hurricane in 1783, restored in 1794, ravaged by hurricane again in 1804, and rebuilt again in 1809 for use by the United States Army. Occupied by the Confederacy during the War Between the States from 1861 to 1865, Fort Moultrie was restored to U.S. Army control as a coastal defense until it was closed in 1947 and became part of Fort Sumter National Monument in 1960. Palmetto logs gave way to brick, concrete, asphalt and steel, but the palmetto tree is still there, flying above the historic site on the state flag.

In the wake of the battle, the palmetto tree became a symbolic fixture in South Carolina, added to the state seal in 1776, and the first coins issued by the state in 1778. In 1861, it was officially included on the first state flag, and finally, in 1939, it became the state tree.

South Carolina's "palmetto flag", featuring a white crescent shape in the upper corner closest to the flag pole along with the tree's white outline centered on a blue field, was adopted by the state General Assembly in 1861 to commemorate symbols that were critical in winning independence.

Many refer to the latter as a crescent "moon", for which there is no specific historical explanation or logical tie, and far more evidence exists to show that the crescent is actually what's known as a "gorget".

Col. Moultrie designed the flag in 1775, and in his memoirs, he describes the banner, referring to its "crescent …in uniform with the troops". He never calls it a moon, and the symbol on troop uniforms he mentions was an upturned crescent worn on regimental caps.

This can be traced more logically to the gorget, which is French for "throat", and was historically a crescent-shaped neck plate on a suit of armor. The gorget became a popular symbol of military rank in the late 1700's, and was a favorite of English King George II, who often rewarded loyal subjects with the upward-turned crescent worn around the neck. One of King George's most loyal subjects was South Carolina Lt. Governor William Bull, who during the 1760's, added the crescent symbol to uniform caps of the state colonial militia, in which William Moultrie served.

Also revealing is the position of the crescent in the original 1861 flag, which still exists, and on which the crescent's open end faces straight up, not at the angle as in the palmetto flag today. Ironically, the original now hangs at the Historical Society of Iowa, whose troops captured the flag from the State House in Columbia in 1865 and have never given it back, but even in the Midwest, it's clear that the intent of the symbol was not to replicate the moon.

As for the palmetto tree, there has never been any doubt as to the steadfast strength and durability it represents, and if there were, all anyone would need for reassurance was a look at any of South Carolina's sea islands after a strong hurricane. The mightiest oaks and pines will snap and give way, but the bending trunk of the our state tree still holds forth under the forceful onslaught as it did so long ago.

Entrance to Fort Moultrie

Opposite: South Carolina Palmetto Tree

GRAVEYARDS & GHOSTS

People may die in Charleston, but they certainly don't go away, and when visitors ask why the grand old houses in the city are so big, the logical answer is that they're built that way to make room for all the lingering ghosts.

Spirits of rebellious slaves, vengeant poisoners, long-lost sailors and jilted lovers are believed to frequent dark alleys, musty attics and creaking staircases throughout historic Charleston, and one of the city's most thriving businesses today is the ghost tour.

Nightly horror tales tell of duelists who return to Philadelphia Alley where they were killed, as well as restless souls of hanged pirates that haunt the city's waterfront. Tortured Revolutionary War prisoners supposedly rattle chains in the provost dungeon of the Old Exchange, while at the historic Aiken-Rhett house, people claim to have sighted ghosts on the

Gravestone with Soul Effigies

formal double stair. A phantom horse and carriage is believed to roam sections of Tradd Street in search of its long-dead owner, and down at 20 South Battery, a headless Confederate is said to linger in hopes of finding

the body part blown off during the Civil War. City legends even include sightings of a dog ghost named Poogan down on Queen Street, which must be terrifying to any cats strolling nearby.

Charleston's melting pot of apparitions includes West African fables of hags and ha'ants. A hag supposedly takes off its skin before entering, or "riding" its victim with terrible pains, and could only be gotten rid of by sprinkling the body with salt and pepper. The term ha'ant, which is commonly mispronounced as "haint", refers to tormenting spirits that invaded homes at night, but were not believed to be able to travel over water. The most famous local ha'ant was known as the Plat-eye, and African descendants in the Charleston vicinity often painted their doors and shutters blue, hoping the Plat-eye would mistake the color for water and go away. Typically, the haunting presence is only as good as the story or the imagination, but in some of Charleston's oldest graveyards, the ghostly specter is sometimes plain as day.

The Circular Congregational Church on Meeting Street boasts Charleston's oldest graveyard, dating to 1680, where one of the most chilling collections of gravestones in America is on display. Featuring hand-carved stones imported from New England, these colonial-era markers are intricately etched with such images as hourglasses, fallen trees, and sunken ships - all symbols of lives cut short. Many are carved with images known as "soul effigies" - combinations of skulls and crossbones, or cherubic faces and wings that represented beliefs and superstitions surrounding the finality and supernatural powers of death.

Unitarian Church

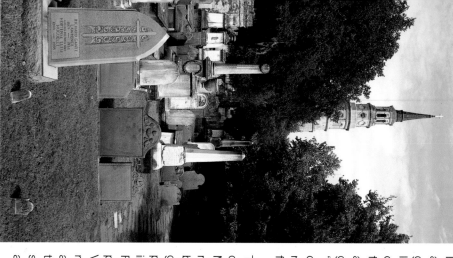

St. Philip's Graveyard

Interment oddities abound downtown, and at St. Philip's Episcopal Church graveyard, a marker shows a skeleton leaning against an hour glass with a cryptic script that reads, "Yesterday for Me, Today for Thee". A few blocks away, St. Michael's Episcopal Church graveyard is the site of the 1770 "Bedstead Tombstone", an 18th-century style wooden marker that resembles a head board and bed frame.

The city's most visual burial ground by day and most frightening by night is Magnolia Cemetery on the peninsula neck. More than 40,000 souls rest beneath huge live oaks and amid the gardens and lagoons of this former plantation, which was dedicated in 1850 as "The City of the Silent". Featuring graves in the shape of pyramids, baby baskets and ornate Victorian sculptures, Magnolia was a regular destination of Charlestonians a century ago, as fearless folks took trolley cars for picnics among the serene statuary where ghost walks are a seasonal event today.

Prevailing attitudes toward ghosts and graveyards have shifted over the years like markers twisted or sunken in Charleston's soft soil, giving more wallop to stories of grave robbers who once plundered coffins with such regularity in the city that interment practices included false, empty graves under which an unmarked corridor was dug to hide the body.

Hiding the dead from prying eyes and hands plays a central role in one of Charleston's most memorable tales from the crypt - the Ghost by the Sea, a forlorn spirit presumably the subject of Edgar Allan Poe's "Annabel Lee". According to legend, a young Charleston girl who died of Yellow Fever in the early 1800's was buried in a deep, unmarked grave at the Unitarian Church graveyard by her father, who disapproved of her lover and never wanted him to find her body. Her ghost emerges from the grave, according to the story, sadly waiting for her lover to return.

Warding off such resurrections may have been on the minds of St. Philip's Church congregation in the early 1800's, when graveyard gates were wrought with skulls and crossbones. Today, St. Philip's still displays a form of ghost-repellant, involving the church graveyard's most talked-about spirit, Sue Howard. In 1987, a tourist's snapshot allegedly captured the image of Howard kneeling over her daughter's grave, more than a century after Sue's death. So many ghost seekers now crowd that spot for a hopeful haunted snapshot that the church installed a marker in front of the Howard grave, telling onlookers that "the only ghost at St. Philip's is the Holy Ghost".

Some visiting Charleston during colonial times literally got a more in-depth glimpse of ghoulishness, falling prey to epidemics that swept the city, earning it a reputation as " a heaven in Spring, a hell in Summer, and a hospital in Fall". So many visitors were victimized that yellow fever became known as "stranger's fever", and the dead were hastily buried in local churchyards as a precaution against spread of disease.

This hurried interment had some legendary and quite creepy consequences. Burial typically included personal effects, which proved a temptation to grave robbers, who discovered that a few folks were put into the ground with such urgency that it was not noticed they were only comatose, as coffin lids sometimes displayed marks of clawing fingers scratching to get out.

The burden on local churchyards was alleviated by a 1768 law designating land on which the district jail was later built as a burying place for "strangers and transient persons", but as late as 1844, the rector of St. Philip's made reference to portions of the church's western cemetery as "adopted as a general burial place for strangers, unknown to this community."

Over the years, St. Philip's burial ground on either side of the

Gravestone with Soul Effigies

St. Philip's Episcopal Church

Philadelphia Alley

church became commonly referred to as the "friendly" graveyard, and was generally set aside for members of the congregation born in Charleston, while the cemetery across the street became known as the "visitors" side, and was more typically reserved for members born outside Charleston.

Even someone as famous as John C. Calhoun, who was a U.S. Senator, Vice President and Secretary of State, was relegated to a visitors side burial in 1850 because he was a parishioner born outside of Charleston. During the Civil War, his remains were moved to an unmarked grave on the friendly side for protection, but after hostilities ended, church members were insistent that Calhoun be put back in his rightful place, where he lies among "visitors" today...or does he?

PATRIOTS POINT & MARITIME HERITAGE

One of Charleston's most visible National Historic Landmarks isn't on land at all, but 33,000 tons of floating steel called the U.S.S. Yorktown. Centerpiece of the hugely-popular Patriots Point Naval & Maritime Museum complex in Charleston harbor, the Yorktown's 856-foot hull does touch bottom, but has been known to drift a bit on flood tides from time to time.

The massive aircraft carrier was brought here in 1975 after its fighting service ended to begin a new chapter in Charleston maritime history. Although representing an era and actions far removed from most of Charleston's seafaring legacy, the Yorktown is a striking example of the kind of living history so unique to this area, and helps rekindle interest in naval traditions that have long influenced the city.

Known as "the fighting lady", the Yorktown went into action during World War II and earned eleven battle stars in the Pacific. She also served in the Korean and Vietnam Wars, and her last duty was the recovery of the Apollo 8 spacecraft in 1970. The interior hangar deck and topside flight deck are packed with more than two dozen vintage aircraft, whose types all served aboard the carrier at one time or another, ranging from bulky World War II Hellcats and Corsairs to aerodynamic F-4 Phantoms and F-14 Tomcats.

One exhilarating experience offered on board is the chance to strap into a Navy Flight Simulator and take controls for a mock dogfight and missile raid, as well as a carrier catapult take-off and an emergency tail-hook landing

Climbing into cockpits of the Yorktown's historic fighters or the seats of its anti-aircraft guns gives a vividly realistic view of the ship's fighting days, but there are also some spectacularly peaceful panoramic views of the harbor and city from the lofty carrier bridge and from the flight command post astern.

Anchored alongside the Yorktown are three other historic ships whose tours through decks, armament and compartments are enhanced by their incredible experiences in service. The World War II destroyer U.S.S.

Laffey survived five kamikaze strikes and three bomb hits within one hour during the battle of Okinawa, and is known as the ship "that wouldn't die". Visitors can walk into gun turrets, along flying bridges and ship's quarters that have been converted into a mini-museum of the naval battles in the Pacific.

The U.S.S. Clamagore is an historic diesel-powered submarine that served from World War II through the Cold War, and was stationed off Cuba at the height of the tense missile blockade in the 1960's. Climbing down hatches leads through torpedo rooms, periscope decks, and engine compartments, and gives the real feel of the unnerving dangers in what was known in Navy parlance as a "thick skin" for its capability for deep dives.

The Coast Guard cutter U.S.S. Ingham, which served more than fifty years in coastal defense and drug interdiction, is one of the most decorated ships in American history, and among the many decorations displayed on its superstructure are decals of marijuana plants for numerous drug busts. There's also a life-size Vietnam-era Naval Support Base on land, featuring attack helicopters and river patrol boats, as well as a museum of the Congressional Medal of Honor Society, citing and honoring the records of all recipients of America's highest military honor from the War Between the States to the present.

Charleston's historic role in maritime history is also well-represented in an unforgettable display of the famed Confederate submarine Hunley at the Warren Lasch Conservation Center along the Cooper River in North Charleston. Lost a few miles offshore from Charleston in 1864 after completing the first successful submarine attack in history, the Hunley was recovered intact in 2000, and today can be seen on weekend tours inside a 55,000-gallon fresh water tank that prevents corrosion. Viewing the amazingly well-preserved 40-foot Civil War vessel shows how far its design was ahead of its time, with tapered hull, flush rivets and skylights, propeller brakes, hydrodynamic conning towers and ballast tanks.

Perhaps the best maritime experience in town is touring Charleston by water, offered on both powered and sailing vessels moored at Patriot's Point and the city's Maritime Center off Liberty Square. Whether it's a dinner cruise, a sunset sail or a trip to Fort Sumter and back, all provide great views of Charleston's steepled skyline and harbor defenses that have ringed the city since the days of pirates.

Fort Johnson on James Island was built in 1708, and it was there that the first American flag was raised to replace a British flag in 1775, and the

U.S.S. Yorktown CV-10

first shot of the Civil War was fired in 1861. Not used for military purposes since 1865, the area is now home to marine research laboratories of the South Carolina Department of Natural Resources

Castle Pinckney, in the middle of the harbor, is a brick fortress built on a small island once filled with orange trees. Although finished in 1797 and equipped with at least one cannon still buried inside, the little bastion never fired a single shot in military action, but was used to house Union prisoners during the Civil War and served briefly afterward as a lighthouse.

Where historic cannon boomed in the open waters between Fort Sumter, Fort Moultrie and The Battery against British, French, Spanish, Union and pirate vessels, today smaller guns start fleets of racing sail boats. Charleston regularly hosts international sailing events, national collegiate championships and local regattas, framed symbolically against the protective background of the mighty Yorktown.

CREEK BEDS TO STREET BEDS

Take a stroll anywhere in downtown Charleston, and there's a good chance you'll be walking on water. More than half the surface area in the old city is "made land", created by filling in marshes and creeks. A number of streets are named after docks, wharves, and waterways on which they were built, and throughout the downtown area, evidence of soggy origins is easy to uncover.

In fact, recent work beneath pavement near the U.S. Custom House uncovered a massive masonry water basin built in the 1850's to keep fish fresh for the market area. Parts of both North and South Market streets follow the course of old Daniel Creek, which began being filled during the early 1700's to connect the town to its first suburbs, and the odd-looking little building just east of the market sheds is an old water-pumping station designed to keep the area from reverting to its original condition after a high tide or heavy rain.

As the name East Bay suggests, the street originally bordered Charleston harbor, and all land to the east has been built atop marsh and mud in the last 300 years. Down East Bay, intersecting streets include Adger's Wharf, Boyce's Wharf, North Atlantic Wharf and South Atlantic Wharf, which is exactly what they used to be. During Charleston's colonial days, long platforms of stone and wood protruded in the harbor where these streets are today, and where cars park now, great sailing ships once docked to unload their cargoes.

Prior to 1740, Queen Street was known as Dock Street because of busy ship traffic on its east end and tidal basin that extended inland as far as Church Street. This explains why the famous Dock Street Theater, first constructed in 1735, now seems misplaced at the corner of Queen and Church streets.

East Battery

The section of Laurens Street leading from East Bay Street to Charleston's Maritime Center was once the city's biggest wharf, along which thirty ships could unload at one time in the 1770's, floating goods down a nearby canal that is now the east end of Calhoun Street.

Farther south, a stroll down the High Battery will still get some occasional salt spray in the eye, but much less so than the days when the location of this raised promenade was a mud bank covered at high tide. To hold back flooding and improve harbor defenses, the city began filling this area during the 1750's. Original barriers of earth, wood and stone were damaged and washed away again and again by tides and hurricanes, and the current structure only dates to the 1890's, when exterior granite walls were filled with stone and brick and bolstered with cement.

East Battery Street passes aptly-named Water Street, which technically lies below sea level and follows the course of former Vanderhorst Creek. Sidewalks on Water Street still display cement posts, called bollards, to which boats could be tied, and crossing this thoroughfare by foot in the 18th century could only be done on a bridge. The hurricane of 1752 pushed a ship so far up Vanderhorst Creek that it didn't run aground until crossing the current intersection at Meeting Street.

A few blocks to the North in sections of today's French Quarter, cobblestone and asphalt surfaces now cover sections of several streets that were tidal marsh in the 1700's and briefly used for rice cultivation, while around the corner at the intersection of Meeting and Broad streets, known famously as the Four Corners of Law, there once stood four corners of a draw bridge, raised and lowered over a moat bordering the original city walls.

Later in the 18th century, a canal was planned along the marshy west end of current Broad Street to connect the old city to the Ashley River. Through this area a "broad path" existed on about the same line as current King Street, on which wagon traffic brought goods from inland past a series of shallow waterways that were converted to mill ponds for rice and lumber production. Other than Colonial Lake, those former ponds now have surfaces of asphalt and grass along Rutledge and Ashley avenues, but remnants of the water-powered era still exist in the West Point and Chisolm's rice mill buildings that serve today, fittingly, as part of the city marina and U.S. Coast Guard station.

On the southern tip of the peninsula was a popular swimming area complete with a bath house until 1911, when 47 acres of oyster banks and mud were filled for a driving and walking promenade now called

West Point Rice Mill Building

ARCHITECTURE, CULTURE, AND NATURE

27

North Adger's Wharf

Jail on Magazine Street. Area that was once mostly marsh has given over the years, and old images of the jail show that the bottom-story windows are closer to the ground than they used to be.

A geodetic survey conducted by engineers in the 1970's discovered that the Charleston peninsula as a whole had sunk some eight inches since the city's founding some three centuries before, and questions arose as to whether it was rising sea levels or too much building on filled land.

The fight to stay above water fits Charleston's embattled tradition. Parts of the city sea wall built in the 1690's can still be seen in the dungeon of the Old Exchange at the eastern foot of Broad Street. The wall was as much for defense against erosion as it was against enemy attacks, and the battle never let up, as 180 years later, the city built military-style revetments on the other end of Broad Street to keep the west side of the city from flooding.

Coping with and conversion of wet surroundings has played a major role in the identity of a city where any location could easily become waterfront with a little excavation. After all, as one legendary local saying proclaims, "Charleston is where the Ashley and Cooper rivers join to form the Atlantic Ocean".

Confederate torpedo-ram CSS David aground at Charleston

Murray Boulevard. This completed years of landfill in a part of the city that may have buried some valuable history along the way. A famous Matthew Brady photograph taken in 1865 shows an abandoned Confederate torpedo boat on mud flats in front of the John Ashe Alston house, where Tradd Street runs today. Some treasure hunters have tried to get city permission to excavate this area to search for the rare vessel, but

U.S. Custom House

considering what's beneath most of Charleston's streets, the torpedo boat has probably long since floated away.

Watery foundations have historically dictated construction methods throughout downtown Charleston, and contributed to some revealing changes in what has been built. Dipping pavement on streets, uneven sidewalks, and buildings with tilting floors are common, as some structures as large as St. Michael's Church are literally floating on layers of clay and tidal drains. Driving pilings and creating other substrata foundations are methods used since colonial times, such as the lengths of red cedar recently found beneath the County Courthouse on Broad Street, but even these can settle if not sunk far enough.

In the late 1790's, for example, a foundation of subterranean brick arches was laid to hold up four stories of thick walls and iron at the Charleston

CHARLESTON'S HAUNTED JAIL

Old District Jail

One of downtown Charleston's most historic and visual sites is largely unknown outside the throngs of thrill-seekers who gather in its sinister surroundings each night. The old district jail, Charleston's "fortress of doom", towers conspicuously over one of the city's least conspicuous locations, a simple housing project on Magazine Street. Opened in 1802, this hulking stuccoed structure held prisoners until 1939, and during that time, little changed inside a grisly lock-up notorious for starvation, overcrowding, disease and torture.

Built atop an unmarked paupers' graveyard that dates to the early 1700's, the jail was designed to resemble a medieval castle, complete with towers, arches and crenelated battlements. For those who would quickly fill its unlighted cells, the primitive penal practices of the day would become as horrifying as any Halloween story, and the jail developed a reputation as stark as the heavy steel bars that still cover its every opening.

Serving a district the size of several current counties, which in the early 1800's included most of the state's population, the jail soon brimmed with a cross-section of debtors, privateers and common criminals. Next door, a "work house" was built in the same style to segregate unruly slaves, but the daily dose of suffering and punishment had equal opportunity in both locations.

Behind hulking sixteen-foot walls, terrors that happened inside the jail stayed inside the jail, unless burial was necessary, in which case bodies were flung in unmarked graves on the outside.

The front steps of the jail were infamously known as the gateway to "Mount Rascal", in which brutal guards would do what they pleased with new admissions that might include free blacks, Federal soldiers during the Civil War, as well as women. Heavy iron doors and gates inside the jail still creak mournful echoes throughout the dark cells and passages, giving life to legends of cruelty, misery, and despair.

Among the most infamous of penal practices carried on in the jail was the "sweat box" or "zipper" - a coffin-like apparatus in which prisoners were made to lie, simmering and suffocating while a lid was nailed on top. In the summers, it was placed outside in direct sunlight with an inmate inside, while during the winter, hot coals where dropped in to make sure the occupant got a warm reception. There was also the "crane" or "crane of pain", which was a device in a small basement cell consisting of two ropes hung from the ceiling, on which an inmate was stretched in the air by the arms and savagely beaten. Placed next to an iron air vent, the crane allowed cries from those tortured to echo throughout the other cells of the jail and create a sense of fear that would keep prisoners in line. With such painful reminders, it's understandable that no escapes were recorded after the crane was put in place.

But the most horrifying and unforgiving jail punishment was the hangman's gallows located in the rear yard. Old newspaper accounts and journals still exist that describe vividly the gruesome details of hangings that took place at the jail until 1911. Along with the crime of murder, horse theft and highway robbery were considered capital offenses in the early 1800's, so there was consistently lots of action at the end of the rope. As if hanging weren't bad enough, the jail gallows was an unconventional apparatus that often left the victim dangling and strangling. Consisting of a vertical beam and crossbar, attached to a pulley through which one end of the rope was placed around the prisoner's neck and the other tied to a heavy counterweight, the execution was performed by opening a trap door beneath the counterweight, violently yanking the victim in the air. Designed to snap prisoners' necks, the gallows didn't always work that well, adding to the host of horrors for those watching from inside.

Jail Yard, Charleston

The terrors of incarceration in the jail are easily conjured up on nightly tours through the cell blocks today. Along with dank, shadowy spaces and bats that fly in from gaps in the rafters, much of the floor and wall area is cracked from age, neglect, and effects of the Charleston earthquake of 1886. The original 1802 cell block and adjoining octagon cell area added in 1855 were both reduced in height as a result of earthquake damage, and supporting steel girders cut through the floors are a reminder that danger still

Portable Inmate Transportation

lurks. Many cell walls are pock-marked with notches made by prisoners counting off the suffering days inside, and graffiti can still be found that dates to the 1850's.

Summer brings stifling heat that causes masonry to drip with condensation, while the 40-inch thick outer walls retain Winter's cold and add to the psychological chill inside dark cells where many poor souls were left to die from epidemics in a facility that, through much of its history, had no running water or interior plumbing. Outside, a rusting iron prisoners' van stands guard over an empty jail yard where hundreds of

Old Jail

inmates once lived in tents due to overcrowded cells, and at night, rustling wind stirs curious sounds that drift from cell windows.

Understandably, the jail is considered one of the most haunted buildings in America, and although many gory stories can't be substantiated, its most famous spirit, Lavinia Fisher, was a person as legendary in life as she was in death.

Arrested in 1819 for her part in a series of crimes that included highway robbery, assault and murder, Lavinia was convicted and sentenced to death. Languishing in the upper stories of the jail for nearly a year as her case was appealed, she took part in a bold escape attempt that involved digging through cell walls and tying blankets together to climb down. Recaptured, she was eventually sentenced to die in a public hanging that drew a big crowd at gallows several blocks from the jail. As her last request, according to legend, Lavinia was allowed to emerge from her cell in her white wedding dress, believing it would make onlookers sympathetic, saving her neck. But as the noose was tightened and she realized there was no reprieve, the evil Lavinia reportedly told the crowd that she would take any messages to the devil himself. Buried in an unmarked grave in unconsecrated ground, Lavinia's restless soul returns to wander the jail, according to legend, as a ghastly apparition in a long white dress, looking for a victim and some revenge.

Accepting the authenticity of Lavinia sightings and other jail spirits gets much better reception inside the old lock-up, where a stale, gloomy darkness has been known to convert even the most determined skeptic. Since the last inmates were moved from the jail nearly seven decades ago, ghosts have had a field day, with numerous reports of cell doors that mysteriously closed, strange footprints that appeared behind locked bars, mournful shrieks and cries heard from upper floors, and unexplained orbs and patterns found on pictures taken inside. With colonies of bats flying in and out of its rafters, and stories of unseen hands that still move old rope-and-pulley dumbwaiters once used to carry food to cells, it's not surprising that trespassing and crime have never been a problem since the jail closed. Whether such reaction represents an over-active imagination or a genuine corridor to a haunted past is debatable, but there is no doubt as to the horrific history that makes this crumbling, empty jail one of Charleston's most intriguing destinations.

RAINBOW ROW

It would not be much of a stretch to say that anyone who has been to Charleston has seen Rainbow Row. This group of historic townhouses on East Bay Street is among the most famous and recognizable images of the city - painted, sketched, printed, copied and sold on cups, hats, placemats, post cards, napkins, towels, t-shirts, books, and magazines in hundreds of places around town.

Yet, all the notoriety is a fairly recent phenomenon, as is the term Rainbow Row itself. For more than a century, these buildings existed in relatively obscurity, and may have been lost altogether, until they got a new identity and a place in history with the simple touch of a paint brush.

All but one of the former merchant's houses from 79 to 105 East Bay Street date to the 1700's, when this section of East Bay Street faced the wharves of a bustling colonial sea port. Built townhouse-style, most with adjoining walls, they were designed to house offices and stores on the first-floor level, with residences above. Businesses included groceries, ship chandlers, mercantile goods, carpentry, as well as offices for factors, an historic term for shipping agents.

Rainbow Row

Rainbow Row

Most of those who built the homes, such as Othniel Beale at number 99-101, lived upstairs with their families. Beale owned a wharf on the other side of East Bay Street, and, after a great fire in 1740 swept the waterfront, designed a double building whose brick walls were covered with a smooth layer of stucco. Besides giving the building an appearance of expensive stone, it conformed to a city fire-prevention ordinance introduced during the 1740's that restricted wooden construction.

When Beale's home stood fast among charred ruins after another great fire in 1778, narrow lots on either side were quickly rebuilt in brick and stucco, and by the turn of the 19th century, the block-long row from Tradd

to Elliott Street was considered such a stylish and prestigious address that number 95 became home to Charles Cotesworth Pinckney, signer of the Constitution, minister to France and Federalist presidential candidate.

For all their colorful history, however, there was little evidence of differing hues along the current row's exterior throughout its early years, and pictures of the area dating into the late 1800's show a drab uniformity of faded neutral tones along the row. Charleston's changing fortunes were often reflected in the facades of its buildings, and in the economic depression after the War Between the States, many buildings along the waterfront suffered from neglect.

By the late 19th century, shipping moved farther up the peninsula to be closer to railroad lines and waterfront near the row began to fill with silt, causing business to dry up as well. Offices were closed, merchants moved their families, and the deteriorating buildings suffered direct hits from both the great cyclone of 1885 and the earthquake of 1886. By 1900, the row of old townhouses was reduced to a literal shell of itself, some gutted for warehouse space, others abandoned and boarded up, while a few maintained small retail spaces as occupying families supplemented income by keeping cows and horses in the open areas in the rear.

It was just such a dilapidated waterfront setting that Dubose Heyward dramatized in his famous 1925 novel Porgy as "Catfish Row", although Heyward's actual inspiration came from a another depressed townhouse grouping two blocks away on Church Street.

The coming of the twentieth century brought some attempts to revive downtown fortunes through urban renewal and included plans by the Standard Oil Company to tear down the Old Exchange, just half a block from the row, to build a gas station. Ensuring concern among local residents that the historic character of the city was being eroded created a surge of preservationist sentiment, and in 1920, the Society for Preservation of Old Dwellings was formed. By city ordinance in 1931, Charleston's historic areas came under protective zoning and a Board of Architectural Review was established. That same year, the old Beale house was purchased by Judge and Mrs. Lionel Legge, who began a restoration that would reveal the architectural splendor along the row hidden for years by layers of paint, wallpaper and temporary construction. Besides the dazzling cypress-paneled interior they restored inside, the Legges decided to give the exterior a fresh new look by painting their townhouse facade in a pastel color, choosing a soft pink reminiscent of the pigments added to stuccos in the West Indies to deflect heat. Just as Othniel Beale had begun a building trend two centuries before, the Legges did the same for the row in the 1930's and 40's. Others began buying the

adjoining properties, restoring many of the original Georgian and Federalist architectural motifs, such as paneled wainscoting and architrave moldings on the inside, while replacing former storefronts and loading passageways with arches, gates, doors and windows. A new identity evolved as more houses were painted with varying shades of exterior color, and Charlestonians began referring to the diverse spectrum of soft pastels stretching down the block as "Rainbow Row", a description that would stick and become internationally famous.

The aesthetic appeal inherent to pastels is their effect of creating visual balance and harmony with adjoining textures and colors, and although the thirteen buildings vary in height, width, and architectural style, the shades of blue, pink, green, mauve and canary blend beautifully with the most eye-catching perspective in a city full of memorable sights.

A symbolic milestone was passed in 1970, with the closing of the last existing business on Rainbow Row - Guida's general store at number 105. But even though the row has been strictly residential since then, it remains a major factor in Charleston business.

Rainbow Row has become an integral part of the city's multi-million dollar tourism industry, as beautification of the line of buildings was a major stimulus to restoration of historic downtown properties that increasingly made Charleston a destination, and led to skyrocketing real estate values throughout the city in the last several decades.

The pastel spectrum is so deeply ensconced in name and image today, that the shade of each building is strictly conformed to under oversight of the now-powerful Board of Architectural Review. Currently, each house on the row is worth millions of dollars, yet as the saying goes in Charleston, a small fortune might you buy a place on Rainbow Row, but only an act of God could change the color.

Rainbow Row

Before Charleston became a major tourist and relocation destination, those growing up amid a downtown filled with historic architecture often took for granted certain treasures such as the city's wealth of wrought iron. Generations of youngsters climbed foot and hand over centuries-old gates, hung rope swings from hand-crafted balconies, or just rattled sticks across delicate garden railings.

Yet back in 1925, one local thirteen-year-old realized an inner passion for wrought ironwork that would win him national fame and recognition, as well as helping revive Charleston's appreciation for the creativity, skill and aesthetic appeal of this timeless art form. Young Philip Simmons landed his first job as a part-time apprentice in a blacksmith's shop on Calhoun Street, repairing wagon wheels for iron craftsman Peter Simmons, who although no relation, formed a lasting impression on his young namesake that would serve Philip well in a career that spanned more than eighty years.

The older Simmons showed his pupil how to work with the iron, to develop a rhythm in striking hammer on anvil, and to realize in the material what shapes he could conceive in his mind. What Philip had in mind would be changed by fate in the thirties, when mass-production of horse-drawn farm machinery and automobile assembly lines drastically reduced the need for hand-forged hitches and wagon wheels, and the number of working blacksmiths dwindled mostly to those who did ornamental work, making the future in iron a rediscovery of its past.

Wrought ironwork in Charleston dates to the early 18th century, featuring decorative varieties forged by assorted early artisans. Meticulously-

21 King Street

detailed shapes lined city streets and became a Charleston trademark by the beginning of the 19th century, and local wrought iron master craftsmen like Christopher Werner became famous for such works as the "Sword Gate" at 32 Legare Street and the balcony and gates of the John Rutledge House at 116 Broad Street.

Hand-shaping by fire and forge was both exhausting and uncomfortable for the blacksmith, and newer technology by the mid-19th century allowed similar shapes to be mass-produced in molten molds of cast iron, so the artistry of wrought iron began to wane.

Simmons had no problem with hard work, and recognized early in his career that old-fashioned wrought iron had a natural artistic and commercial niche in traditional Charleston. He set out on his own to revive a more personal touch in wrought iron and began building a clientele by offering to make whatever concept the customer wanted. These ideas he sketched first on paper included birds, snakes, stars, fish and other

Wrought-iron replica of Luther's seal to mark the 250th anniversary of their first communion service at St. John's Lutheran Church by Philip Simmons

intricate shapes that would test his artistic skill. Putting concept to reality in hard iron on the anvil was a grueling process of blistered hands, aching muscles, and scorched skin - and there was no guarantee anyone would buy into what had been in vogue more than a century before, but Simmons' work was on the money.

The work he did daily for decades was remarkable in endurance alone. The first task in wrought iron is softening shapeless pieces by shoving them into white-hot in coals. Heated to a fiery glow, the iron is quickly pulled from

Gazebo at Charleston International Airport designed by Philip Simmons and Mary Edna Fraser

the coals and placed on an anvil, where powerful strokes with a bulky hammer creates the new contours of twists, tapers and points. Much of the blacksmith's skill and suffering comes from the need to hover over the scorching heat to make sure the iron is just the right temperature for shaping. Pounding iron that is heated too much or too little can ruin it, and the best gauge, according to Simmons, is to keep one hand on the cool end protruding from the coals.

Entrance to Charleston Visitors Center designed by Philip Simmons and Mary Edna Fraser

John Rutledge House Inn

Opposite: Sword Gate by Christopher Werner - 14 leaves replaced by Philip Simmons

Double Heart Gate designed by Philip Simmons, fabricated by his cousin Joseph Pringle and nephew Carlton Simmons

Snake Gate by Philip Simmons

St. Philip's Episcopal Church

He is undoubtedly the most acclaimed master craftsman of wrought iron in Charleston history, and the city has honored his timeless contributions with creation of two special gardens that feature his unique designs. The Philip Simmons Heart Garden on Anson Street is entered by a remarkable double gate wrought in the shape of a heart, and includes a topiary designed by internationally-acclaimed arborist Pearl Fryar. The Philip Simmons Children's Garden on East Bay Street honors the master ironsmith with a

Iron work with gas lantern

Yet for all the rough nature of wrought iron, Philip Simmons at work was the picture of ease and efficiency, striking blows in a ringing rhythm with hands that never seemed to hurry, strain, or suffer. The joy he got from doing the work was obvious, and seemed to be much more satisfying than the accolades that came as his career flourished. He learned that the term "artist" didn't bring customers, but that the key to success in iron work was to give people what they wanted, whether it was forging the customer's design or his own interpretation to suit the most discriminating tastes. Time has proven that the uniquely lively and pleasing concepts that Simmons could convey convincingly in iron were exactly what people wanted, and today, more than 500 of his creations grace houses, gardens and courtyards all over the city.

St. Philip's Episcopal Church

Diligently productive and dedicated to his art for decades, Simmons has been recognized with a Heritage Fellowship award by the National Endowment for the Arts, given the Elizabeth O'Neill Verner Award for Lifetime Achievement in the Arts, inducted into the South Carolina Hall of Fame, awarded South Carolina's Order of the Palmetto, as well as rewarded with an honorary Doctorate in Fine Arts from South Carolina State University. His public exhibits include works at the South Carolina State Museum, the Richland County Museum, the pool gate at the Governor's mansion, and the entrance gates to the Federal Courthouse in Columbia. The National Museum of American History of the Smithsonian Institution purchased a gate Simmons made on the Mall of the Lincoln Memorial for inclusion in their collection, and Brookgreen Gardens in Murrells Inlet has a garden gate of his design.

Washington Park

life-size bronze sculpture of him at work, surrounded by enticing examples of his concepts, such as an ornate butterfly trellis. The Philip Simmons Park near his birth place on Daniel Island is that community's municipal park, and features the island name gilded in gold that Mr. Simmons forged at age 89.

Yet for all his success and the hard, physical life he endured, Philip Simmons' most enduring legacy has been the gentle, unpretentious joy of his work, his teaching and his inspiration. Volunteering his time to teach aspiring ironsmiths at the American College of the Building Arts, regularly speaking at area schools and churches, and celebrated throughout the city for his positive contributions, Philip Simmons' name embodies the exceptional quality of the iron he has wrought - a lasting gift to the city of Charleston.

Philip Simmons Park at Daniel Island. Ironwork by Philip Simmons

CHARLESTON BY THE SEA

Surrounded by the fabled "Harbor of History" as well as pristine expanses of coastal wildlife habitat, Charleston is as impressive by water as it is on land.

One of Charleston's most visual traditions is its fleet of shrimp trawlers - the high-bowed, flat-bottomed boats topped with wing-like outriggers that pull nets filled with the city's favorite marine morsel.

A majority of the trawler fleet docks along Shem Creek, just across Charleston harbor in Mount Pleasant, where harvesting from the water has a mixed and storied past.

Salt was produced in Shem Creek as early as the 1860's, as shallow depressions were dug in marshes just above the high tide mark to trap water that would evaporate in the sun and leave a mineral residue. During the 1890's, part of the creek was used as a "cooter pen", in which terrapins were beefed up on diets of fiddler crabs and shipped to fancy restaurants up North. After World War One, crabs were processed and oysters canned at Shem Creek processing plants.

For many years, shrimp were harvested around the creek by throwing and dropping nets, but that business and Shem Creek fortunes changed dramatically after the building of the Grace Memorial Bridge across the Cooper River in 1929. Trucking replaced freight boats in Charleston harbor, and captains began converting their vessels to trawlers, dragging weighted nets through schools of brown and white shrimp.

With Shem Creek's advantageous proximity to the harbor channel and offshore shrimping grounds, the first trawler dock was built there in 1930, and since then, the shrimping fleet has dominated the creek shoreline with a distinctive look that has become one of the biggest tourist attractions in the area. On board, things haven't changed that much over time, as methods and machinery that did the job more than 75 years ago are pretty much the same today.

A typical day aboard a shrimp trawler begins about 4 a.m., as diesel engines are fired up and boats move off into the darkness while crews

Shrimpboat at Crosby's Fish & Shrimp

Trawls must be pulled in a straight line at about 3-4 knots, just fast enough for water flow to trap sea life against the nets, but slow enough not to rip nets open. Because there's no way of seeing what's going on or in the nets below the murky surface, a smaller "try net" is dragged behind the trawler and pulled in from time to time to make sure shrimp are there, being caught.

Brown Pelican

gobble fried eggs, grits and bacon in the cramped galleys. The first few rays of sunlight cast silhouettes against the brick walls of Fort Sumter as the trawlers chug their way out of the harbor and past a break in channel jetties known as Dynamite Hole.

Pelicans awaiting an easy dinner

Local oysters

By sunup, the shrimp boats are a few miles offshore, swinging outriggers to each side and lowering huge 20-fcot nets into the sea for the first of a long series of trawls.

Keeping nets spread out during the trawl is critical, and is done by lowering flat, wooden "doors" inside the nets' outer edges so that the buffeting force of water will hold them open side to side. To keep them stretched from top to bottom, a buoyant "float line" keeps the upper side of the net on the surface, while a weighted "foot rope" or "tickler chain" drags the lower end across the bottom, kicking marine life up into the net.

Shem Creek

Depending on the trawler captain's experience and instinct as to when the catch is full, nets are winched in and dumped on deck. A good trawl will yield hundreds of pounds of shrimp, as well as assorted fish and crabs called "by-catch". Although most trawler nets are equipped with excluder devices that allow other species to escape, it's not uncommon to have flounder, spot, drum, blue crabs, and an occasional small shark in the pile of shrimp on deck, so gathering the catch can be a challenge.

Oyster Harvester

Everything marketable is packed on ice, the rest is swept over the side, and the trawl begins all over again. It's a familiar sight from Charleston beaches as the trawlers rock slowly side to side, with nets straining in their wake. Where there are shrimp trawlers, there are likely to be flocks of sea gulls and pelicans overhead and pods of dolphins and porpoises behind, as they have learned that nets in the water mean a meal is nearby.

When a shrimp trawler returns to Shem Creek at the end of the day, the success of the catch can usually be measured as easily by the wake of creatures that follow right up to the docks.

Blue Heron

Another seafaring group of gatherers that made its mark on local folklore was the "Charleston Mosquito Fleet". This legendary flotilla of simple hand-made boats existed in various form from the early 1800's to the 1930's, as generations of poor, local fishermen sailed dugout canoes and dories from wharfs on Charleston's east side far into the open sea for catches of red drum, shrimp, flounder and mackerel. Rigged with collapsible masts and colorful hand-sewn quilts and sheets for sails, mosquito fleet boats usually carried oars on board just in case they ran out of favorable breeze. Known for their daring and skill in regular daily

trips that might take them beyond the sight of land, the fleet brought back fresh seafood to the city market and for cart-pushing vendors to hawk on Charleston streets, singing out to houses as they passed. Ironically, modern fishing boats and techniques like trawling made the mosquito fleet obsolete.

Other old-fashioned methods have survived in gathering lesser quantities of seafood, as shrimp, mollusks, crabs and fish are still caught around Charleston waterways by a variety of nets, hooks, spears, hands, shovels, hammers, tongs, and traps, while some creatures have simply jumped in boats by themselves.

"Scratching" for clams continues to be a tradition in the area, as harvesters wander mud banks at low tide with baskets and trowels, searching for a small depression, or "key hole", that shows where the clam has burrowed. Digging bent over for hours at a time, the scratcher will earn about 12 cents per clam, so it's not a job many are seeking.

Into similar mud flats, oyster gatherers plod to scoop up and break off masses of shells. Beneath the layers of oysters, stone crabs burrow in holes, where catching requires some nerve to reach in with a bare hand to scoop the critter out without losing a finger to powerful claws. These crushing claws are a delicacy that will regenerate, so the accepted practice is to take one off and throw the crab back.

Another old favorite is "gigging" or "graining" for flounder at night with bright lights and long spears, or "gigs" in shallow water. The lights attract the fish, which can camouflage themselves by changing pigments in their scales to match the surrounding bottom, so expert giggers learn to spot the outline of the fish in the sand or mud. Besides a good eye, gigging takes a good aim, as refracted light in the water can make the target look closer than it is. Charleston's catching tradition goes on among the wildlife world too, as brown pelicans make dramatic headlong dives for fish, egrets and herons stand with graceful patience to pounce on crustaceans, and schools of mullet rip the surface in nature's ceaseless chase.

And even for those not after prey, just catching a glimpse of Charleston's seaside spectacle is worth a trip to any of a bevy of local beaches at Sullivan's Island, Isle of Palms, Folly Beach, or Kiawah and Seabrook Islands.

Egret

Opposite: Blue Crabs

EARTHQUAKE BOLTS, STUCCO & OTHER EXTERIORS

One of the great delights for youngsters growing up in old Charleston houses was to make the walls of the building into a sand box. All they had to do was scrape away at some of the aging stucco exterior to reduce the mixture of lime, water, and sand back to its original components, and no one who has done it has ever forgotten the trouble it got them into.

Stucco has been a favored Charleston construction material since the earliest days of the city. It was cheap and relatively easy to maintain, provided a weather and fire repellant, and could be shaped to resemble stone to give residences a more expensive look.

In 1720, Col. Robert Brewton's house at 71 Church Street was the first in North America to be adorned with decorative stucco quoins, French for "corners", which were textured to look like marble blocks. This colonial fashion statement presumably was for anybody who didn't realize how wealthy the Colonel already was, and set a Charleston standard in surface styles for more than a century.

Brewton's house and stucco still stand, as do many buildings that appear to be made of solid stone, but are actually covered by thin layers of

Earthquake Bolt

stucco, hiding more basic building materials beneath. City Hall on Broad Street, for example, was constructed as a bank in 1801, and originally displayed a red brick exterior with marble trim. In 1882, white stucco was added to the bricks, in what may have been the first official cover-up authorized by city politicians. Farther down Broad Street at the Old Exchange, the beige exterior hides more brick, flanked by true Portland marble quoins that only a trained eye can distinguish from the stucco variety.

Throughout the colonial period, bricks were mass-produced in kilns around Charleston, often resulting in poor-quality "soaker" bricks that absorbed moisture and deteriorated easily. Stucco proved to be an effective remedy to problems with brick, which could easily be layered with this protective masonry skin that was often pigmented with colored sand or burnt clay, and given texture by adding binders of straw or animal hair. Stucco was made even more durable late in the 19th century by additives that included blood, urine, eggs, beeswax, whiskey and beer to fortify consistency, strengthen adhesion, and prevent shrinkage and water absorption that sometimes broke down the older mixtures.

Broken walls became a major local concern in 1886, when the city was staggered by a violent earthquake that knocked down buildings, killed 92 people, and severely damaged much of the downtown area. Charleston, it was discovered, lies on a crack in the earth's crust known as the Woodstock Fault, and in the ensuing era of rebuilding and repair in the late 1800's, many structures were fortified with a new architectural oddity, the earthquake bolt.

Because the tremors had caused most destruction in the form of cracked and crumbling walls, the post-earthquake technology bound buildings together with stabilizing rods built horizontally through floors and tied off

Chevaux-de-Frise

on opposing exteriors with oversized nuts and washers technically known as "gib plates". With Charleston's proven preference for show-off exteriors, the exposed bolts, or plates, soon became a fashion statement, and along East Bay Street and the High Battery alone, houses can be found sporting such shapes as stars, crosses, and lion's heads on brick and stucco facades.

Although considered completely useless by engineering standards today, earthquake bolts still adorn houses throughout Charleston, and have become were such an integral part of the city's architectural tradition that recent restorations and reproduction houses have added faux bolts and plates without the interior connecting rods, just for the look.

Earthquake Bolt.

Another exterior addition that shook things up in Charleston's past was the seal or badge of fire insurance companies, known as a "fire mark". Charleston fire insurance companies date to 1735, oldest in America, and each company originally had its own fire brigade. Fire marks indicated a substantial monetary investment in a building's safe-keeping, and although fire brigades would respond to and help fight any fire, there were reward incentives to save buildings with marks on the exterior wall.

Even fire marks couldn't save nearly 300 Charleston houses burned in the great fire of 1740, after which the city passed an ordinance prohibiting wooden exteriors. Although that law eventually vanished, the fire marks did not, and oval plaques made of cast iron or lead eight to ten inches in diameter inscribed with historic fire brigade logos can still be found on facades around the old city.

One famous facade marked dramatically by fire insurance, or lack of it, is the Cathedral of St. John the Baptist on Broad Street. The Victorian-era Gothic church replaced another cathedral that burned on that same spot in another terrible Charleston fire in 1861. The earlier church, completed in 1854 as the Cathedral of St. John and St. Finbar, featured a similar Connecticut brownstone design topped by a 200-foot steeple. However, fire insurance on the church had lapsed only weeks before it burned, and what money could be raised to begin rebuilding in 1890 ran out by 1907, minus the planned replacement steeple, giving the current church a somewhat crew-cut appearance.

Charleston Fire Insurance Company's "Fire Mark"

Earthquake Bolt

actually molded acorns, but the "Acorn Gates" just doesn't have the same ring.

To say the array of Charleston exteriors is colorful would be no understatement, especially considering the years of confusion caused by a hue known as Charleston Green. A common shade on historic gates, doors and shutters throughout the city, Charleston Green is a peculiar pigmentation with a unique origin. The story local folks like to tell is that black paint donated to the heavily-damaged city by the Federal government after the Civil War was a bit too much for proud Charlestonians to accept, so it was "purified" by adding a hint of yellow. To this day, it takes a seasoned eye or a touch of sun to distinguish this color from black, and there are still minor battles waged here and there over exact tint of replacement paint.

Another historic exterior form throughout the city is the piazza, which is Italian for "square", but in Charleston means a colonnaded porch or veranda running the width or length of the building. Designed on most "single" houses to give shade from afternoon heat and sun on the south side, piazzas are typically within earshot of windows next door. This architectural arrangement created a cultural tradition known in Charleston as "northside manners", which means refraining from the temptation to eavesdrop on the neighboring piazza to the south.

Some piazzas around town are adorned with a not-so-polite addition known as Chevaux-de-Frise, consisting of a long iron bar surrounded by sharp, protruding spikes. Literally translated to mean "horses of Friesland", this device got its name and fame in 18th-century European wars as an effective barrier against cavalry charges, and became popular in Charleston as a security measure after an aborted slave uprising in 1822. Built horizontally or vertically on structures where an intruder might climb, the grisly apparatus is displayed most noticeably on gates at the Miles Brewton House at 27 King Street.

Cathedral of St. John the Baptist

Considerably less sinister is the pineapple symbol carved or molded on gate posts, doorways and walls around the city. Pineapples were considered a rare, luxurious delicacy in colonial America, and became symbolic of wealth and welcome, particularly in the city named for English King Charles II, who included the pineapple in his official portraits. The most famous of these, the "Pineapple Gates" at 14 Legare Street, are

GETTING TO KNOW CHARLESTON'S BOTTOM

Charleston is surrounded by bodies of water on and around which many significant events have occurred over the centuries, but for all the illustrious past above the surface, there's quite a story to be found underwater as well.

A wealth of submerged historic artifacts lie on river and estuary bottoms throughout the Charleston area, well-hidden by the local phenomenon known as "black water". The name refers to a dark, tea-like color caused

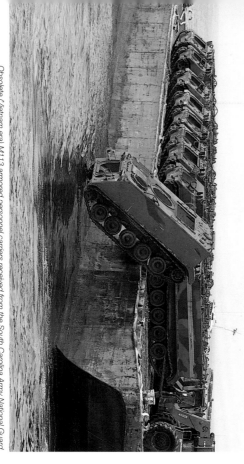

Obsolete (Vietnam era) M113 armored personnel carriers received from the South Carolina Army National Guard. These carriers are located on the Jim Caudle Memorial Reef, the Charleston 60' Reef and the Edisto 40' Reef.

by silt and decaying organic matter suspended in the water as it flows down stream. Viewed from the surface, black water visibility extends only a matter of inches, and below the water, even scuba divers are swallowed in darkness only a few feet down. Yet that intimidating gloom has produced some illuminating finds.

Probing the depths blindly as well as with high-powered underwater lights, divers have opened an unexpected window to the past with a wealth of

discoveries that date as far back as dinosaurs and prehistoric times. Large shark teeth, whale bones and other fossilized remains are regular finds for black water divers in the Charleston area. Thousands of years ago, the entire coastal plain of South Carolina was a seabed, beneath fathoms of salt water in which huge prehistoric creatures swam. As the sea receded over the centuries, those creatures died and many of their remains were buried in the layers of bottom sediment that eventually became dry land. Today, the scouring action in stream channels caused by heavy rains and rising water levels continuously exposes these ancient artifacts.

Diver on artificial reef

With the coming of humanity, rivers became transportation arteries and dumping areas, and mixed in with dinosaur bones are well-preserved canoes, flatbed rafts and sailing ships from centuries ago. Many man-made artifacts have been brought to the surface and used to piece together the history of ancient Indian tribes that settled the Charleston area, as well as giving clues to the colonial period. Yet there's enough stuff under the water for people to learn first hand, and one section of the Cooper River near historic Mepkin Abbey has been designated by the state as an Underwater Heritage Trail, complete with markers and written descriptions below the surface for inquisitive divers to find. The trail features a number of artifacts, most notably cargo vessels from the rice plantation era, still mostly intact at depths of 15 to 20 feet.

Charleston Soda Bottle

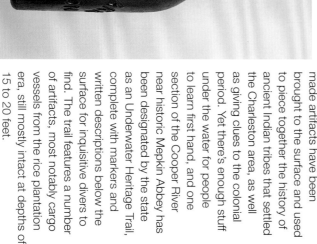

South Carolina Dispensary Bottle

Getting in touch with history in black water bottoms doesn't have to be a major underwater undertaking, but it does take some nerve. One method used to explore the darkness requires only a scuba tank, a flashlight and a screwdriver. Down at the channel base, water flow can be overpowering, so the screwdriver is tied to the diver and stuck into the mud to hold against the current while the flashlight is held in one hand, freeing the other to grope for artifacts.

Besides the lack of "viz", other dangers can lurk in the form of sharks, alligators or entangling, sunken debris, so a good light, a savvy partner and a quick escape route are all considered critical for safe searches.

Findings can be as varied as the diving experience, as some turn up a wealth of Civil War buttons and bullets or colonial china and silverware, while some show bottoms full of nothing more than Budweiser bottles. Actually, bottles are a common sight and often very valuable, as finds vary from hand-blown "onion" bottles and mechanically-pressed perfume bottles dating to the 1700's, to "Jo-Jo flasks" and jugs of the South Carolina Dispensary from 1893-1907. The latter group comes from the fourteen-year period when the state controlled all sales of alcoholic

Onion Bottle amd Black Ink Well

South Carolina Dispensary Bottle

Stoneware

beverages and required liquor bottles to be embossed with a palmetto-tree logo. Whether or not the Dispensary system had any effect on liquor consumption or taxation is debatable, but it certainly changed the nature of state river bottoms, where numerous reminders of white lightnin' are now filled with black water, and have provided so much treasure that some expeditions could be called "fire water" dives.

One of Charleston's most notable displays from the past that actually surfaced on its own is the massive whale skeleton that hangs from the rafters of the Charleston Museum. The bones are the remains of a right whale that inadvertently swam into Charleston Harbor in 1880 and couldn't find its way out, so the mammoth mammal may be a lasting testimonial to the visual limits of the black water perspective.

Visibility clears dramatically just a few miles offshore, where the flow of particulate matter that darkens the rivers begins to dissipate and sink. Surprisingly, the ocean floor just off Charleston features an abundance of reefs that brim with bright coral and schools of sea creatures. Most reefs are man-made, either the result of old shipwrecks to which coral has attached, as well

South Carolina Dispensary Bottle

Megalodon Shark Tooth

Mastodon tooth (prehistoric elephant)

Megalodon shark tooth

All artifacts and fossils are from the private collection of John Taylor.

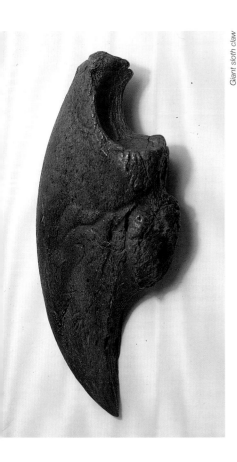

Giant sloth claw

the year. Changing water temperatures attract an ever-revolving menu of cobia, amberjack, sheepshead, tuna, sea trout, grouper, mackerel, spadefish, pompano and shark.

But even in this relatively clear area, some of the best finds are hidden. Such was the case of Charleston's most famous artifact, the Confederate submarine Hunley, which was thought to have been destroyed in 1864, but was lying there four miles off shore all the time. Layers of sand and mud had packed atop the famed sub, creating an anaerobic seal that kept the vessel remarkably well-preserved and intact for 136 years beneath the surface.

So, even though water around Charleston doesn't always sparkle with clarity, its visual potential should not over overlooked, and with some extra effort and curiosity, there's no telling what historic highlight might come to the surface.

57

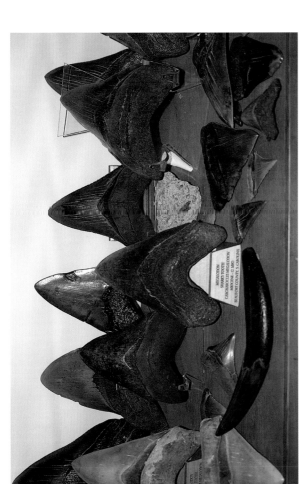

Collection of shark teeth

Whale vertebra

as a recent state program that has intentionally sunk everything from concrete bridges to obsolete U.S. Army tanks to extend the reef habitat.

Sinking environmentally-safe steel and concrete in select offshore areas around Charleston has turned 20 square miles of lifeless sand into what's known as "live bottom", where sponges, corals and other invertebrates attach to hard surfaces and begin the food-chain that attracts swarms of fish.

At depths ranging from 20 to 110 feet, visibility can be very good, and scuba divers find octopus, barracuda, anemones and sailfish among the diverse underwater population. The popularity of reef diving has increased with the number of sites to explore, and the thrill is enhanced by viewing opportunities that may range from remains of old sailing ships to very lively hammerhead sharks.

Anywhere there's real activity below the surface, there's real activity above it, and offshore reef-fishing near Charleston is very popular throughout

MEMORABLE VS. MYTH

In an old city like Charleston where so much history is narrated every day, facts are sometimes exaggerated and frequently argued, and tour guides say that amateur historians can be found on any sidewalk, waiting to pounce on renditions of the past that differ from their own. Many versions of Charleston's history have been passed down by word of mouth from people who've long since departed, so there's bound to be a little variation that no one can prove either way. Still, what has some basis in fact can easily be separated from other tales that are blatantly untrue.

One of the most notoriously erroneous local myths is the frequently-told story that symbols of bulls' and rams' heads built on the Market Hall exterior were put there to indicate the presence of meat markets to illiterate slaves. That story is pure baloney, however, as images of bulls and rams were popular motifs of the Romanesque architectural style that influenced Charleston architect Edward Brickell White's 1841 design. Temples in ancient Rome commonly displayed carved animal heads symbolizing sacrificial offerings, and during the Roman Revival period of the mid-19th century, such ornate construction details were widely used on buildings ranging from libraries to monasteries.

A similar yarn claims the "hat man" painting on the side of 47 Broad Street was put there to entice hat buyers who couldn't read. The image, consisting of a grinning individual with body parts made of hats, was painted in the late 1800's when the site was occupied by a hat outfitter, the C.C. Plenge Company. In truth, such scene-depicting signs were

The Pirate House, 145 Church Street

very common for Charleston businesses since the 1700's, and included images of clocks, boots, apothecary mortars, coffins and horseshoes to display the obvious wares and skills inside. As for the idea that the images were for the illiterate, another sign long-displayed on Broad Street across from the Hat Man was a likeness of Ben Franklin's head, a traditional motif indicating a book store.

Another entertaining, but fabricated story is the legend of the pirate's walk and tavern at 141-145 Church Street, where stories say outlawed buccaneers tunneled beneath the city during colonial times to secret hideouts where their money was welcomed by illicit merchants. The unfortunate fact is, any subterranean passage beneath Charleston's muddy foundation not dug 30 feet down into the hard marl would quickly fill with water, and although parts of a demolished tavern on Broad Street were brought to the Church Street location to add to existing construction, there's no evidence that there was ever any genuine pirate or tavern on this spot.

One of the most commonly convoluted claims is the extent of blood and gore from duels fought on Philadelphia Alley, where losses at Gettysburg would pale in comparison. Although duels were fought there and in other parts of Charleston from the early 1700's until the state outlawed the practice in 1880, few if any died, and honor

was usually satisfied when participants were slightly wounded - commonly known as being "pinked" in colonial vernacular - or if pistol shots missed entirely. Still, the practice was enough of a problem that an Anti-Dueling Society of Charleston was formed, and addressing that group in 1828, Roman Catholic Bishop John England lamented that dueling's "temporary madness" was plaguing the city.

Other frequently-heard Charleston myths include:
- The idea that "single" houses were built sideways to the street to reduce taxes on frontage. In fact, the design was intended to keep houses cooler in the tropical climate by facing protective piazzas into the sun and creating airflow along open space the length of the structure.

Opposite: Two Meeting Street Inn.

- A misconception that the area bounded by East Bay, Cumberland, Meeting and Broad streets was historically known as the "French Quarter". In fact, the neighborhood was not called by that name until 1973, when the term helped focus preservation concern over a planned condominium project.

- The belief that the cannon now on display at The Battery took part in the initial firing on Fort Sumter in 1861. In truth, none of the guns that are there today were at The Battery at any time during the Civil War, and those that were on the site in 1861 were not powerful enough to reach the fort.

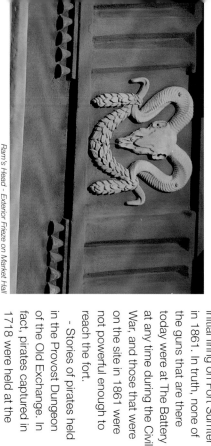

Ram's Head - Exterior Frieze on Market Hall

- Stories of pirates held in the Provost Dungeon of the Old Exchange. In fact, pirates captured in 1718 were held at the same location, but in a building called the Court of Guard that was later torn down. Construction of the current building was begun 1767, and completed in 1771. The basement area known as the dungeon was actually built as a storage area for shipped goods, and was not used to imprison people until the British occupied the city in 1780.

- Legends that three large oaks in the Charleston Jail yard on Magazine Street were hanging trees. In truth, these oaks were mere saplings when the last hanging took place at the jail in 1911. Historic pictures and drawings of the jail yard show no evidence of the trees as recently as the late 1800's.

- Beliefs that slaves were sold at the city market area, whose historic wares were meat, vegetables and produce. During the slavery era, sales and auctions were held on street corners along East Bay Street just north of the Old Exchange, until an 1856 law required that all sales be held in private venues, such as The Old Slave Mart at 6 Chalmers Street.

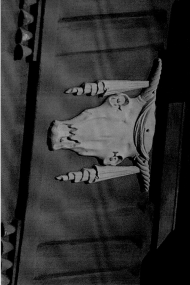

Bull's Head - Exterior Frieze on Market Hall

Sometimes, what's true about Charleston is as mystifying as myth, most memorably:

- The fact that the wall around St. Michael's cemetery was completed in 1816, after the church sexton was admonished "not to let horses and cattle graze in the church yard".

- Curbing on many Charleston streets was made from lumber in the 19th century, but had to be replaced with stone and slate after much of it was stolen for firewood.

- Before the advent of steam power in the early 1800's, some of Charleston's rice and timber operations were powered by windmills, including a 100-foot spinning tower at the current northwest corner of Colonial Lake.

- St. Michael's steeple was painted black during the Civil War so that it would be harder for bombarding Yankee gunners on Morris Island to sight in as a target.

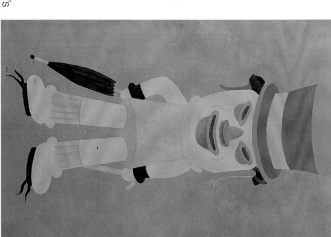

Hat Man painting at 47 Broad Street

The City Market

second story window during a reception at 106 Tradd Street, and returned to his plantation to recover, thus avoiding capture when the city fell. Legend says he chose this exit in order not to cause an embarrassing scene when his loyalist host offered a toast to the King.

- The outstanding Queen Anne style house at 2 Meeting Street was built in 1892 from a $75,000 wedding present left by a wealthy Charleston banker to his daughter on a satin pillow.

- The cupola atop the Col. John Ashe house at 32 South Battery once served as a lighthouse for ships entering Charleston harbor.

Old Exchange Building and Provost Dungeon

Old Exchange Building - Sea Wall

Old Slave Mart

- Charleston's oldest municipal building, the 1713-era Powder Magazine on Cumberland Street, proved to be a much better wine cellar than it was a storage area for gunpowder.

- A section of Broad Street near Meeting was paved with wooden bricks in the late 1800's to soften the sounds of passing traffic so as not to interfere with proceedings at federal and county courts nearby.

- Construction of stone jetties in the 1880's to protect Charleston Harbor was supervised by U.S. Army engineer Quincy Gillmore, who had tried to destroy Charleston's harbor defenses as a Union commander during the Civil War.

Of course, many old Charleston stories are difficult to prove or disprove, and will remain legend, such as:

- The reason for Francis Marion's leap to freedom in 1780. As British troops besieged Charleston, the man who would become the "Swamp Fox" broke his leg after jumping from a

The Powder Magazine

VIEWS, NOOKS & CRANNIES

From almost any perspective in downtown Charleston, there's something that can't be seen anywhere else in the country, and many of these visual experiences are completely free.

Getting some of the best looks at Charleston takes extra effort, such as views from the hiking and biking lanes across the towering new Arthur Ravenel bridge that straddles the Cooper River. Atop the longest cable-stayed bridge in North America, with a clearance of 175 feet over the harbor channel, are spectacular, unobstructed views of the historic city, sea islands, Fort Sumter and Castle Pinckney, Patriot's Point, cruise liners, sailboats and huge container ships passing beneath.

Other spots, such as the corner of East Bay and Tradd streets, only require a turn of the head to see Rainbow Row, the High Battery, Charleston harbor, the Old Exchange, cobblestone streets, and the only point on the peninsular city with a view all the way from the Ashley River on the west to the Cooper River on the east.

Off the beaten path are a number of historic walking alleys worth a look, such as Stoll's Alley off East Bay Street, which features a number of Philip Simmons' gates, as well as stunning colonial gardens along the way, and in places is so narrow, someone could climb by simply pushing against opposing walls. From Church Street, a stroll down tiny, rustic Longitude Lane actually

Longitude Lane

takes an east-west latitudinal path past historic houses and gardens until it intersects Latitude Lane, which, ironically, runs on a north-south longitudinal axis.

Over on Meeting Street, the Gateway Walk extends from the famed Circular Congregational Church, across three blocks and two streets through the grounds of the Gibbes Museum of Art, past the Charleston Library Society, and through lush greenery and rare flowers behind

Fireproof Building

antebellum houses into the spooky, and supposedly haunted Unitarian Church graveyard on Archdale Street.

Philadelphia Alley, in the French Quarter, is legendary as the city's dueling alley and passes the historic Footlight Player's theater and St. Philip's Church graveyard, while Unity Alley between State and East Bay streets is a charming passageway that includes historic McCrady's Tavern, where visitors can share the same dining area where George Washington sat in 1791.

From the gates of old Washington Square at Meeting and Broad streets, various vantage points offer picturesque views of the historic Four Corners of Law - City Hall, built in 1800 (municipal law), St. Michael's Church, built in 1761 (God's law), the Charleston County Courthouse, built in 1787 (county law), and the Federal Courthouse complex, built in 1896 (federal law). On the other side of the park, a there's a view of three unusual

Stolls Alley

structures with a common fiery legacy - the Palladian-style Fireproof Building, built in 1827 of stone, glass and metal to be resistant to blazes; an old city bell tower, constructed in 1880 to ring out fire alarms; and the Greek-Revival Hibernian Society Hall, built in 1840, where the revelry of Irish toasting traditions has long burned brightly among this benevolent brotherhood.

Facing Hibernian Hall is an historic view of Charleston's most famous cobblestone thoroughfare, Chalmers Street, whose surface is so bumpy that an old local yarn claimed that pregnant women often conceived after driving down the block. Ironically, there was a baby store for a number of years at the east end of Chalmers, where notable sights today are the Old Slave Mart and the Pink House, a colonial tavern that dates to the early 1700's.

Stepping out of hot sun or rain on the brownstone-columned porch of the Dock Street Theater on Church Street offers one of Charleston's most classic views in the form of the famed English Renaissance steeple of St. Philip's Church, whose columns and portico extend out into Church Street, supporting a bell tower that served as a harbor range light from 1893-1915. Across from the theater are the Gothic Revival spires of America's only French Calvinist, or Huguenot church, a congregation whose services were once scheduled according to tides for the sake of parishioners traveling by boat from inland plantations. A step back inside the Dock Street lobby shows a detailed reconstruction of the first building designed specifically for theatrical purposes in America, in 1735. Nearly a century later, the theater was converted into the Planter's Hotel, where this same lobby featured a fashionable drink that would become famous as Planter's Punch.

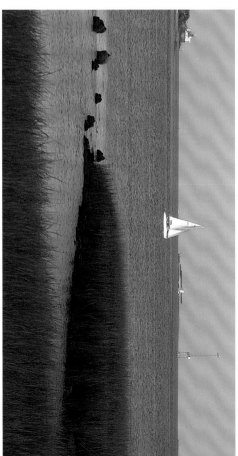

Charleston Harbor

Opposite: South Battery

Farther west on George Street, the historic College of Charleston features one of America's most picturesque campus centers at Randolph Hall, which dates to 1828, and was used as a backdrop for memorable scenes in the movie "The Patriot".

Renovated with a magnificent Ionic portico in 1850, Randolph Hall stands over a massive outdoor cistern, where graduations and Spoleto events have been held, and for which the complex is known. Surrounding the cistern are towering live oaks, historic wrought iron fences, and antebellum buildings that include a Romanesque triumphal arch, making it one of the great lingering locations in the city.

Only a few blocks away on Calhoun Street is Marion Square, still dominated by the turreted walls of the State Arsenal built here in the 1820's. In 1843, the arsenal became home to the South Carolina Military Academy, now called The Citadel, which moved to its present campus in 1922. Today, the arsenal building is a hotel, but is highly-visible as a historic reminder along with a towering statue of famed South Carolina statesman and orator, John C. Calhoun; remnants of tabby walls built to defend the city during the Revolution; a Holocaust memorial; as well as monuments to state military heroes Wade Hampton and Francis Marion, the "Swamp Fox" for whom the square is named.

Once a popular gathering spot where folks watched Citadel cadets take their marching drills, Marion Square's block-sized expanse was also home to air shows in the early 20th century, as dirigibles and hot air balloons landed in what is now a valley of serenity among the heart of Charleston's chic urban shopping district, where today's biggest show is people-watching. Citadel cadets in uniform still put on a great spectacle with public parades on Friday afternoons at the current campus near Hampton Park.

Washington Park

College of Charleston

Another lingering locale good for taking in both Charleston's old and new is from the steps and portico of Market Hall on Meeting Street. Elevated high over the entrance to the city market and painted in florid colors, this 1841 Roman Revival building is hard to miss. From various points along the wrought iron balustrade, there are excellent views down four historic streets, across to majestic Charleston Place, and beside one of the liveliest outdoor market venues anywhere. A step inside the building will actually cost a few bucks, but the United Daughters of the Confederacy Museum is a must for the Civil War crowd.

Just around the corner on Hasell Street are book-end views of two of Charleston's most historically and architecturally-significant houses of worship. On one side, the Classic Revival beauty of Kahal Kadosh Beth Elohim houses the oldest synagogue in continuous use in America, while across the street, Tuscan-porticoed St. Mary's is the mother church of Roman Catholicism in the Carolinas and Georgia, featuring historic ceiling and gallery paintings.

No tour of the city is complete without a stroll through Waterfront Park, at the foot of Vendue Range. With grand views overlooking Charleston harbor, the park lies on the remnants of old wharves where ships once brought waves of people who shaped the city's past, and is highlighted by a massive fountain shaped in the form of a pineapple, a traditional symbol of welcome.

DOLPHINS, PORPOISES & TURTLES

Since Charleston's founders splashed ashore in 1670, there's always been a fascination with what comes out of the water, and more than three hundred years later, the show still goes on.

The aquatic acrobatics of local dolphins and porpoises are legendary as they make a spectacle of themselves in ship channels, along beaches, and in rivers and creeks. From vantage points around Charleston harbor, they can be seen hurtling bow waves pushed by passing freighters, and the beach at Sullivan's Island near Fort Moultrie is one of the best spots to observe these creatures swimming close to shore, chasing schools of prey. Often flinging their bodies through the air in great vertical spins or horizontal arcs, these frolicking fins are friendly, unless of course you're a fish, and although sometimes mistaken for sharks, local dolphins and porpoises are rarely distinguished from each other.

Coming from the same family as whales, both are air-breathing mammals with long, gray bodies, round heads, fins, flippers and flukes, who communicate and navigate by projecting sound waves underwater. Generally dolphins have a protruding beak, and thus the name "bottlenose", and porpoises are slightly smaller, but the only consistent difference is that porpoises have big, spade-shaped teeth, while the dolphin's choppers look like pointed cones. They both make a series of noticeable noises that sound like clicks, whistles and laughter, and are vocalizing with mouths that gape open at the surface. In fact, the sound actually comes from air being exhaled from a blow hole on their backs.

Easily capable of swimming 30 miles an hour, submerging for twenty minutes and diving as deep as 900 feet, dolphins and porpoises are amazing under water, but some of their best antics take place where anyone in the Charleston area can see. One is called "tailing", a

splashing frenzy in which the creatures seem to be standing on their heads in shallow creeks and bays. They're actually probing for fish hiding in murky bottoms, thrashing their tail flukes back and forth to push their mouths into the mud. Another eye-catching, fish-catching method is known as "stranding", in which dolphins and porpoises swim at great speed up on to a beach or sand bar, pushing a wall of water and fish in front of them, before eating the stranded prey and wiggling back into the surf.

Their reputation for friendliness actually comes from curiosity and appetite, as dolphins and porpoises that ply coastal estuaries will frequently surface alongside boats and docks, and will happily gulp down any fish thrown their way. Unfortunately, feeding them is illegal in South Carolina, so it's better to enjoy the spectacle with eyes only.

Another out-of-water experience in the Charleston area that is more environmentally serious than for show is the summer migration of the loggerhead sea turtle. From mid-May through August, these massive creatures will emerge from the ocean to lay eggs on area beaches, and although an incredible event to witness, it's one that's best left alone.

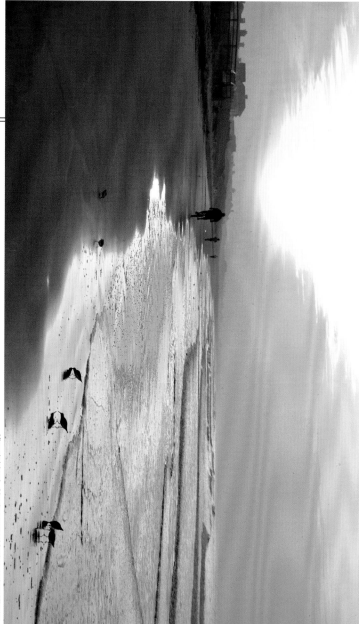

Kiawah Island - Nesting ground for Loggerhead Turtles

incubation period of about 55-60 days, patrols can usually predict and be ready to help when nests come to life with the second phase of this regeneration.

Once a clutch begins to hatch, a surge of tiny turtle bodies works its way up through the sand, and swarms of brownish heads and flippers clamber over each other in a frenzied instinct to get out and crawl back into the sea. Loggerhead life begins vulnerably, with a soft carapace about the size of a silver dollar that beach crabs and other predators will pounce on and gobble up along the way to the surf. The turtle patrols help protect hatchlings at this stage by scooping them into buckets and carrying them to the water's edge, where they're released and swept by incoming waves into the relative security of a realm in which they'll spend the rest of their lives.

Sadly, nature claims most of these delicate, weak creatures, and only about one in ten thousand will survive Atlantic Ocean storms, predators, drowning, and starvation to reach adult size.

Dolphins

Feeding on plankton at first, then crustaceans and fish, the few that do make it have little limit on how big they can grow and how far they can go, having been known to swim into the southern hemisphere and back in a life that may span fifty years. With luck and a little help from humans, a few of these tiny turtles may return much bigger to South Carolina's coast years from now for the same purpose, attesting dramatically to the strength of nature's instinct and its capacity for survival.

Loggerhead Turtle

The loggerhead turtle is an air-breathing, sea-dwelling reptile that must lay its eggs in warm sand in order for heat to incubate them. Reaching sizes as big as 300 pounds or more with an outer shell, or carapace, as much as four feet long, the loggerhead is a good swimmer, but is vulnerable on land, so laying activity is always at night, under the cover of darkness. The dunes of Charleston's surrounding sea islands have always been favored laying spots, but scientific studies show that loggerheads will avoid coming ashore at all if beaches are too well-lit, so "lights out" programs go into effect each summer to help keep dwindling loggerhead populations intact.

Some observation is necessary, however, in documenting this protected species, and just north of Charleston at the Cape Romain National Wildlife Refuge, marine biologists and seasonal volunteers carefully monitor and oversee laying activity, offering a helping hand to new hatchlings in the process.

Roaming refuge beaches silently each night during the summer, these groups look for ruts in the sand that indicate a turtle has surfaced and lumbered its way inland. Following the crawl to the creature, lights are turned off and no sound made, as the slightest human interruption could cause the turtle to turn back into the ocean and dump its eggs to die exposed in salt water.

For thirty minutes or more, the loggerhead will flail awkwardly into the sand with its giant rear flippers, slowly hollowing out a hole about eighteen inches deep. It's an exhausting exercise for an animal so clumsy out of water, and the turtle will gasp audible sighs as, one by one, eggs finally drop in the hole. The group of eggs, or clutch, numbers about 100 or more, with leathery, white surfaces that look like ping pong balls. When done laying, mama loggerhead sweeps sand over the eggs, pounds it down with the underside of her shell, and turns to crawl back into the sea with glistening eyes that legend says are tears shed for offspring she'll never see again.

Because high tides can ruin the loggerhead's nest, which is also susceptible to raccoons that dig and feast on the yolks, patrols dig them up and move eggs to hatcheries farther inland, where they're covered by sections of fencing. Here, eggs are reburied alongside other clutches laid on different nights, and marked by number and date. With the average

CHARLESTON'S LEGACY OF RICE

A famous old saying in Charleston was that people who grew up here were like the Chinese, because they worshipped their ancestors and ate so much rice. In fact, Charleston's ancestor worship was a choice, but the consumption of rice was pure necessity.

Not so long ago, meals in Charleston typically consisted of breakfast in the morning, dinner at midday and supper at night. Breakfast could be anything from hominy and eggs to sliced tomatoes, and supper could vary from boiled shrimp to peanut butter and jelly sandwiches, but dinner always included white rice and gravy. This was never the boiled or fried variety, but puffed to a supple consistency by steaming with water.

Such was the tradition that began in the late 1600's, when lands around the city then known as Charles Town were planted with rice seeds from Asia and Africa, and grew to such economic importance that the yellowish color of the husk was only part of the reason it became known as "Carolina Gold".

From a subsistence crop of 10,000 pounds in 1698, the Charles Town area was exporting 20 million pounds of rice by 1730, aided by favorable geography, climate, politics and supply of labor. Early planters discovered that rice did very well in wet soils, and cleared 150,000 acres of tidal swamp in and around Charles Town for seeds which flourished in hot, humid summers.

Benefitting from the work force of a thriving colonial slave trade, planters soon realized that Africans from places like Sierra Leone and Gambia had long been skilled in growing rice, and many of these imported concepts were used to greatly enhance production. Essential to the African rice crop was a cultivation technique that took advantage of tidal flow along coastal rivers, as earthen dikes were built to create fields that could be flooded or drained to irrigate the crop and kill competing weeds. This simple, ancient method, which is well-displayed in exhibits at the Charleston Museum, featured a series of wooden structures known as "trunks" and "gates", through which water flowed and levels could be manipulated to enhance cultivation.

Africans also helped introduce the effective step-by-step process of converting a harvest of wet stalks into finished barrels of rice. First, they would dry husks and remove from stalks by heaving in the air with long-handled flailing sticks, then grind with a wooden mallet called a mortar in a bowl known as a pestle to break the kernel from the skin, and finally separate the desired grain by shaking loose on wide, flat baskets in a process known as "fanning".

When the English crown relaxed trade and tax restrictions on rice shipments during the 1700's, the crop created enough wealth to make the young city among the most prosperous and influential in America, and it was largely the profit from rice that established the social and architectural legacy of historic Charleston.

Opposite: Carolina Gold - stalk of rice

Heyward-Washington House

Original cobblestone street, Chalmers Street

The city's most notable colonial-era structures, including St. Michael's Church, the Old Exchange, the County Courthouse, Rainbow Row, and the Heyward-Washington House, were all afforded by the fortune of the rice-based economy. Even buildings where the rice was milled reflected the earnings that rice produced, and the Italian Renaissance facade of the 1845 Bennett Rice Mill on Concord Street has been preserved for its reputation as the finest example of 19-century American industrial architecture.

Not only did rice shape the city with the opulence of wrought iron, slate sidewalks, and grand piazzas, it also contributed, indirectly, to our cobblestone streets. Rice was so valuable during the eighteenth century, that owners of sailing ships entering the harbor would load hulls to the brim, often dumping their ballast of heavy stones on Charles Town wharves for added cargo space. By the 1770's there were enough cobblestones lying around to pave many of the city's muddy, gravel streets with the bumpy surface on which several thoroughfares still wear out shock absorbers today.

Middleton Place Rice Mill

Most of the famed plantations and plantation gardens around Charleston achieved their grandeur through wealth from the rice trade, and in the 1700's, sea-faring ships sailed up the Cooper River as far as Berkeley County for priceless cargoes. A number of area plantation sites still display

Flood Gate at Caw Caw Interpretive Center

remnants of mill chimneys and steam-powered machinery used in rice production, and most are bordered by dikes and impoundments that once surrounded rice fields.

Interior of Middleton Place Rice Mill

The need for slaves to work the crop brought a large influx of West Africans who greatly influenced Charles Town's character and culture, while the moneyed rice-plantation class emerged as a potent political force that would help shape a new state and nation, as three of the four South Carolina signers of the Declaration of Independence were rice planters.

Rice maintained a strong economic role here until early in the twentieth century, when a series of destructive hurricanes and cheaper competition from the Southwest put Lowcountry South Carolina rice cultivation out of business, but the grain retains a strong local influence. In many fields where rice once grew along rivers outside the city, the trunk and gate system is still used to generate seasonal grasses that greatly enhance wildlife habitat, and makes South Carolina's coast one of the continent's most environmentally-important areas for winter waterfowl migrations.

Most hard to change, however, was a taste that has been savored for more than three centuries in Charleston, and although dinner is a night-time tradition around here now, rice still holds a regular place at the table.

COOPER RIVER BRIDGES

*F*or more than seventy-five years, the best view in Charleston has also offered the city's most inexpensive thrill - standing on a lofty perch atop bridges across the Cooper River.

The city was deep into its third century before the Cooper was first spanned by a bridge, and George Washington himself was among the countless souls who had to be rowed or ferried to make the trip over from the Mount Pleasant side. The distance across the Cooper from peninsular Charleston is about two miles to the east bank, where a former form of river fording can still be seen just north of Patriots Point and the U.S.S Yorktown. Still visible just above the waters' surface, is the hull of the S.S. Archibald Butt, an early twentieth-century steam ferry that lies proverbially stuck in the mud. The fact that the S.S. Archibald Butt is named after an American military officer who went down with the Titanic lends greater symbolism to this lost chapter in Charleston history.

When Teddy Roosevelt's "Great White Fleet" steamed up the Cooper River in 1912, the line of mighty battleships was the greatest display of modern engineering ingenuity yet seen in Charleston, but by the roaring twenties, the era of automobiles brought another technical marvel that would dominate the river and the surrounding landscape.

The John P. Grace Memorial Bridge would become the most ambitious construction project Charleston had ever seen. Stretching more than three miles, the steel and concrete bridge arched steeply 150 feet above the Cooper River ship channel and 135 feet over the nearby Town Creek channel in its path from Mount Pleasant to the city. Both sections that crossed shipping lanes were supported only by double-cantilevered superstructures from above, creating separate thousand-foot long roadbeds seemingly

suspended in mid-air. The cantilever system maintains the strength of an arch by creating stress in opposite directions, with the steel superstructure serving to double that force, and in the case of the Grace, forged a distinctive steel latticework more than 200 feet high.

Built from opposite ends inward, the bridge was riveted together piece by piece, placed into position by huge 400-ton cranes that rode on special tracks along the steep grade. Beneath the bridge, foundations were imbedded deep into the river bottom, as swirling water was held back by massive caissons that extended well below the water line.

Grace & Pearman Cooper River Bridges

Opened in August, 1929, the bridge had two opposing lanes of traffic, and each crossing cost a 50-cent toll. The narrow ten-foot lanes took such a dramatic rise in grade that the bridge was soon nick-named the "world's longest roller coaster", and at first, some cars had to be towed due to engines overheating while making the climb.

Fear was a factor when crossing above mammoth ships whose masts and smokestacks were so high that they sometimes barely missed the roadbed, and drivers were spooked by stories of a ship that did take out a section and several cars in 1946, as well as the legend of workers buried alive inside the huge bridge supports when concrete was accidentally dumped on them as they dug the foundation.

The Grace bridge was not nearly as intimidating as it was an avenue of great change. The new link to the north helped tourism become a major factor in Charleston, increased trucking and other business, and paved the way for development of Mount Pleasant, Sullivan's Island and the Isle of Palms.

In 1966, a second double-cantilevered structure, the Silas N. Pearman Bridge, was built alongside the Grace to share the traffic load, and Charleston briefly boasted the longest one-way bridges in the world. For most Charlestonians, the bridges were rarely called by their given names, but referred to as the "old Cooper River bridge" and the "new Cooper River bridge". The image of dual skeletal superstructure would eventually become world-famous, however, not for the vehicles that drove it, but for the feet of those running across.

The Cooper River Bridge Run that began in 1978 with about 700 participants is now among the most prestigious road races in the world, and draws an annual contingent of more than 30,000.

The great draw, besides a chance to visit Charleston in the Spring, was the challenge of the steep roadway and the incomparable view up on top, and in less than 30 minutes, a good runner today can complete a journey that took cars about the same amount of time in the 1920's and 30's.

Yet for all the millions who crossed the Grace bridge and the tremendously advantageous impact it had made on Charleston, relentless reports that it was unsafe and obsolete finally led to construction of the cable-stayed Arthur Ravenel Bridge in 2003, and dismantling of the older structures.

The Ravenel bridge was built higher to accommodate the very largest of container ships, and features a main channel clearance of 186 feet with a span extending 1546 feet. Also built much wider, the bridge has eight driving lanes as well as separate pedestrian and bike paths.

Unlike suspension bridges such as the Brooklyn Bridge, whose roadway is suspended from vertical cables attached to supporting towers, the Ravenel Bridge supports the roadway by cables attached directly to the anchoring towers, each 575 feet high, making it more efficient and less prone to damage or need of repair.

The size and accessibility of the Ravenel bridge was an instant success, and hundreds of joggers, bikers and walkers wander across each day for the spectacular view.

Today, the original Cooper River Bridge is gone, but ironically, sentimental interest toward the old Grace has raised it much higher in public opinion than it ever enjoyed when it was a working highway. Books and documentaries have been devoted to its history, pieces of the Grace have become collectors' items, and it seems that everyone in town now has some fond memory along its steep, narrow lanes.

The truth is that the old Cooper River Bridge did change Charleston's look then as the new bridge affects the local perspective today, and no one who ever crossed either will forget the experience.

Ravenel Bridge, foreground with Pearman and Grace Bridges, background

GLORIOUS GARDENS

Long before carriage tours, ghost walks, and harbor cruises, the biggest draw for tourists in Charleston was its gardens. For centuries, the city has flourished with resplendent color in remarkable settings throughout the downtown area and in all directions beyond, and no place in America can compare to Charleston in full bloom.

Azaleas

At Hampton Park in the northwest section of the city, a circular drive around banks of azaleas and moss-covered live oaks follows the path of the old Washington Race Course, a horse-racing facility built in the 1790's. During the Civil War, the infield area of the horse track became a temporary prison for thousands of Union soldiers, and in 1901, the grounds were converted into a fantasy landscape of elaborate white buildings known as "Ivory City" for the Interstate and West Indian Exposition, a world's fair concept intended to draw business to Charleston. Although the Exposition was a failure and the Ivory City soon torn down, a pleasant landscape, reflecting pond and sunken gardens remained for public use in a park named for former governor Wade Hampton in 1903.

Acres of flourishing greenspace would serve briefly as a football field for The Citadel nearby, later as a city zoo, and today as a spacious picnic and recreation area that includes the Noisette Study Garden reserved for unusual species of roses.

At the other end of the city, White Point Gardens features some of the city's most impressive stands of azaleas under a canopy of towering oaks and palmettos, surrounding a classic Victorian bandstand that is a favorite for outdoor weddings. Bordered by rows of white and red oleanders

along the High Battery and Murray Boulevard, the peaceful park setting was initially created by a city ordinance in the 1880's that set up turnstiles to keep out "cows, mules, horses and inebriates", and although that barrier is long gone, today's visitors don't have to share space with grazing cows.

Perhaps the best location to take in Charleston's panorama of gardens is along downtown sidewalks from late Winter to early Summer, stopping every few steps in front of gates, driveways and alleys to admire the colorful spectacle within. Besides pink, white and red azaleas, there are the rich hues of camellias, jessamine, magnolia, hydrangea, bignonia, hibiscus, tea olive, syringa, and wisteria, to name a few. Although these are generally on private property, with occasional signs reading, "please enjoy the view from the street", the eyes can't trespass, and most Charleston gardens are designed to be seen easily by passersby.

Cypress Gardens

Many of the city's historic homes were specifically designed to include the enticing symmetry of formal gardens. The Nathaniel Russell House at 51 Meeting Street, for example, was built in 1808 and is famed for its magnificent Adamesque interiors and free-flying staircase, yet a pleasurable part of this museum house tour is to linger amid garden

Drayton Hall

Nathaniel Russell House Gardens *Charleston*

Opposite: Boone Hall Plantation

Camellia

Magnolia

Surrounding Charleston are numerous antebellum plantations famed for their grounds and gardens.

Magnolia Plantation and Gardens off U.S. Highway 61 boasts the oldest estate garden in the western hemisphere, begun in 1680. A former rice plantation, Magnolia's cultivated area was converted for a more florid form of planting in the 1840's by owner John Grimke Drayton, an Episcopalian minister, who was fascinated with horticulture and introduced the first azaleas to America.

blooms beneath majestic magnolias for a seat on one of Charleston's classic "joggling boards" - a long, flat beam of cypress or heart pine pegged to rockers on either end for a bouncing, swaying ride that has been a staple in downtown gardens for hundreds of years. The Russell House is home to the Historic Charleston Foundation, whose annual Festival of Houses and Gardens has been for more than sixty years a tremendously popular event in Spring, when the city comes alive with color.

Lady Banksia Rose

Over on U.S. Highway 52, Cypress Gardens is essentially a flooded forest of giant cypress trees set in a blackwater swamp, surrounded by banks of blooms. The water is so-called because of the tannic acids released by leaves and is actually so pristine that it attracts a host of plants, mammals and reptiles that are easily viewed from walking paths or by small boats that can be rowed through the gardens area.

Also noticeable throughout the gardens are the prevalent cypress "knees" that protrude like sculptures from the water. The reason for these unusual growths remains a mystery, although it is believed that they anchor the towering trees in the soft swamp bottom.

East of the city in Mount Pleasant, Boone Hall Plantation is an antebellum indigo and cotton plantation whose stunning avenue of oaks dates to 1743, and has been used as a backdrop in a number of movies. Still a working plantation, Boone Hall has seasonal U-pick harvests of strawberries and pecans. The old plantation grounds feature butterfly gardens and historic slave cabins along pristine salt marsh creeks where crops were once loaded for shipment to Charleston.

Gazebo at White Point Gardens

Reverend Drayton created the famous reflecting ponds that enhance the natural beauty of Magnolia Gardens today, as well as footpaths, wooden bridges and banks of flowers whose dimensions are doubled in the glassy surface of the water. Magnolia Gardens also features a separate Barbados Tropical Garden devoted to exotic plant species, and the Audubon Swamp Garden, a wetland natural habitat filled with wild plants and animals.

Nearby Drayton Hall features hundreds of acres of marsh and river walks beneath ancient live oak trees. Listed as a National Trust Historic Site, the 1740-era plantation mansion is the oldest surviving example of Georgian-Palladian architecture in the South, having escaped burning during the Civil War by what legend says was a clever ruse. In 1865, invading Federal troops from Sherman's army burned

Wateria

most of the plantation houses along the Ashley River, but spared Drayton Hall because the owners allegedly convinced the Yankees that it was a smallpox hospital.

Farther down highway 61 is Middleton Place, a National Historic Landmark and home to Arthur Middleton, a signer of the Declaration of Independence, who is buried in a great tomb in the midst of the gardens area. Sixty-five acres of ornamental garden – are highlighted by terraced "butterfly lakes" overlooking the Ashley River.

Sadly, the great plantation home, which dated to 1741, was burned by Union soldiers during the Civil War, leaving only the southern flanking wing intact. This part of the original house overlooks the symmetrical designs of gardens designed in the 1740's to include meticulously-manicured "allees", or walkways, whose trees and shrubs create natural partitions for flowered galleries.

Opposite: Middleton Place

CANNONBALLS, PIRATES & THE BATTERY

For all the bristling displays of guns and ammunition around Charleston's White Point Gardens, which is commonly known as The Battery, the only damage they've done in nearly 150 years is to those who've climbed on and fallen off. Flanked by banks of azaleas, oleanders and a grand harbor view, the obsolete arsenal has been a relaxed sightseeing fixture for so long that many a visitor asks if indeed any of the weaponry is real.

In fact, some of the hardware here never fired a shot in anger, but collectively, what stands silent today represents some of the most volatile episodes in Charleston's and United States history.

Originally, this southernmost tip of the city's peninsula was a muddy shellbank known as Oyster Point or White Point, where colonial fortifications were first built to protect against threats from the sea. Although settled by the English, the city was initially not part of a royal colony and not protected by the British fleet, so during Charleston's early history, pirates such as Blackbeard, Anne Bonny, and Stede Bonnet often made harassing visits.

Like the current "show" guns of The Battery, the few that were placed at Oyster Point didn't scare off buccaneer ships that lurked in coastal inlets and frequently pounced on shipping outside the harbor entrance, but another showy edifice did. In 1718, forty-nine pirates, including the notorious "gentleman pirate" Bonnet, were captured and hanged on gallows built along the current Battery. Left swinging on

ropes to rot in the sun, the dead pirates dangled for weeks as a grisly warning to others not to attack the city again.

Today, a granite marker along the South Battery section of White Point Gardens indicates where the pirates were believed to have swung, but the gallows themselves have long disappeared like many guns that have served at this spot.

During Charleston's early years, batteries of cannon placed along Oyster Point fought mostly high tides and hurricanes until the War of 1812, when more protective barriers allowed the guns and the nickname "Battery" to stick, and with it, a legacy of defensiveness that was sometimes literally over the top.

Keokuk Gun

In 1865, for example, evacuating Confederates blew up a massive Blakeley gun mounted at The Battery to keep it from falling into the hands of advancing Union troops. Part of the big cannon fell instead about two

hundred yards away into the roof of 9 East Battery, where it is still lodged in the attic today, and is a reminder of one local tongue-in-cheek saying that guns at The Battery caused more destruction to the city than to attacking forces.

At the same spot where the Blakeley gun was launched, today the corner of South and East Battery, sits a huge Civil War cannon that was brought here by the U.S. Navy to bombard the city, but ended up being used by Charleston defenders to fire back. The eight-ton Dahlgren gun was aboard

Dahlgren Gun

the U.S.S. Keokuk, part of the Federal ironclad squadron blockading Charleston, when it was sunk in shallow water off Morris Island by Confederate cannon on April 7, 1863, its twin gun turrets still protruding above the waterline.

Under the cover of darkness in succeeding weeks, local engineers sneaked under the noses of the Union ships to pry open the turrets and remove both big guns, placing them at area fortifications for use against their former owners. Lost after the war, one was found in 1899 and placed at its current location to face new groups of invading Yankees each tourist season.

On the same row farther down East Battery are three symbols of battlefield endurance against terrible odds and withering fire. Two are twin Columbiad cannon that were mounted briefly at Fort Sumter during

Rifled Cannon, foreground with Seacoast Mortars, background

suddenly wanted it back. When one enterprising soul got the city to agree to purchase and replace the gun with a newly discovered "sister", the Longitude Lane crowd went into battle, demanding "our cannon or no cannon" and won a prolonged fight with City Hall.

Stuck with the replacement weapon, the city decided to mount it at White Point Gardens, where historians had a little problem with its claimed Revolutionary War status. Close inspection shows a bit of pipe protruding from inside the muzzle, and because the technology of cooling hot layers of metal around pipe to form a cannon barrel was first used in the 1840's...well, it's still only a little more inconsistent than what's next along Murray Boulevard.

The four massive guns along the southern edge of the gardens are seacoast mortars used during and after the Civil War to lob huge shells into ships and fortifications, against which crushing power was as deadly as explosives. Next to each is a pyramid-shaped pile of ammunition which looks impressive but wouldn't work much better than the Longitude Lane gun. These are 10-inch diameter surplus cannonballs, while the mortars' barrels were designed for 13-inch projectiles.

Defending positions around the rest of White Point Gardens are a World War I howitzer, a French 4-pounder, a Spanish-American War rapid-fire gun, as well as a rifled cannon and a bronze howitzer from the War Between the States. Whether or not any saw any action on any battlefield is dubious at best, but their ability to put the hurt on climbers is well-documented.

Phony Revolutionary Cannon

Live Oaks at White Point Gardens

bombardments that reduced the fort to rubble, while between them is a statue of Gen. William Moultrie, who along with the statue of Sgt. William Jasper on the alley behind him, represent the heroic defense of Charleston during the Revolution.

Around the curve to the South on Murray Boulevard, is a weapon that created much more fuss than fire. What looks like a nine-pounder from the Revolutionary War is actually a fake, but did ignite what was known as the "War of Longitude Lane". Back in 1935, city workers removed from the little alley off East Bay Street a half-buried iron obstruction that turned out to be an old cannon - much to the dismay of residents who

CHARLESTON LIGHTHOUSES

The shifting sand bars surrounding Charleston harbor have been a magnet for boat bottoms since the city's first settlers went aground more than 300 years ago, as many a local mariner has experienced an unexpected high and dry.

Safe channels from sea to shore are constantly changing and hard to see in the murky water, and until the advent of sonar depth sounders and bathymetric technology, lights and landmarks were crucial to Charleston shipping.

There are two historic lighthouses on barrier islands flanking the mouth of Charleston harbor. The Morris Island tower dates to 1876, and has stood against the ravages of time and nature to become one of the most famous lighthouses on the Atlantic coast. The Sullivan's Island light, built in 1962, was once the most powerful beacon in the Western Hemisphere, and is still in service, seen clearly 26 miles at sea.

Lighting up the harbor entrance dates back to 1690, when the life's blood of the early royal colony was a sea trade that could not afford to sit stuck or sunk in sand. An act was passed in Charles Town in 1673, providing for wooden towers to be built on Sullivan's Island and manned by watchmen who would light baskets of pitch and oakum to mark the channel entrance.

By 1700, other colonial provisions were established to "make the channel more remarkable to mariners". One such method was the clearing of underbrush and low growth near a stand of towering trees on James Island, known as "One Hundred Pines", to give day-sailors an easy reference point.

The most visible signal, day or night, was a strong light, and after a series of small, primitive range beacons were set up around the harbor entrance during the early 18th century, Charleston's first true lighthouse was built on Morris Island in 1767. Designed by Samuel Cardy, whose other towers included St. Michael's church, the 42-foot tubular brick construction featured a burning lamp of whale oil or lard. Strengthened and heightened during remodeling in 1802, the light served the city until a more powerful, revolving beacon extended aid to navigation from a new 102-foot tower in 1838.

The second Morris Island lighthouse was an easy target in the midst of what became a major battlefield during the War Between the States, and was completely destroyed. It wasn't until the end of Reconstruction that a 161-foot brick tower was again raised on Morris Island, withstanding severe hurricanes, a major earthquake, occasional water spouts, and even a few near-misses during World War II bombing exercises.

Built on an eight-foot thick base atop piles driven fifty feet into the marl, the tower on Morris Island was known as the Charleston Main Light and was active for nearly 90 years. Painted with black and white horizontal striping that distinguished it from patterns of other lighthouses along the South Atlantic coast, the Morris Island light served as a day-marker for

Morris Island Lighthouse

Morris Island Lighthouse

vessels as well. Advances in optical technology during the mid-1800's allowed for stronger beams of light, and thus higher towers were built to extend beyond the curving earth. The Morris Island light is a dizzying nine stories of iron spiral staircase, which would give a stiff "lighthouse leg" to those who had to climb up and down to trim wicks and carry buckets of whale oil. At the top is a "lantern room" with an incredible 360-degree view of the Carolina coast, as well as an exterior iron parapet that was ringed with downward-focused lights during the 2002 Spoleto Festival as a "shining" example of site-specific art.

The Morris Island light was originally equipped with a state-of-the-art Fresnel Lens, in which light from burning wicks was intensified and magnified inside a cylinder of rotating lenses. Twelve feet tall and weighing three tons, the lens cast a beam visible more than fifteen miles. Although no longer in service, the Morris Island lens still holds its position along the South Carolina coast, yet in another lighthouse…but we'll get back to that later.

The eventual decommissioning of the Morris Island lighthouse came not as much from obsolescence as from erosion, which, ironically, was more influenced by mankind than by nature. In 1878, the U.S. Army Corps of Engineers began construction of separate stone jetties - one starting on Sullivan's Island and the other from Morris Island - that would extend 14,000 feet almost completely submerged to flank the harbor channel. Built by sinking log mattresses loaded with stone, the jetties were intended to funnel the flow of ebbing tide along the channel to scour the bottom and maintain depth. Modern hydrologists have found that, along with channel silt, the jetties have been responsible for washing away a huge chunk of Morris Island.

In 1880, for example, the Morris Island lighthouse was 1200 feet from the shore, and fifteen adjacent buildings, including a one-room school house, served the three keepers, known as "wickies", and their families. By 1938, rising water had washed away all the buildings and lapped at the foundation of the lighthouse, forcing the Lighthouse Service to relocate the wickies and replace the historic Fresnel lens with one that could be automatically controlled.

Sold at auction, the lens eventually ended up as property of the Friends of Hunting Island Lighthouse in Beaufort County. That lighthouse was designed to be taken apart and relocated in event of erosion, which it was in 1889, and today it sits high and dry, displaying the Morris Island lens for any visitor to see.

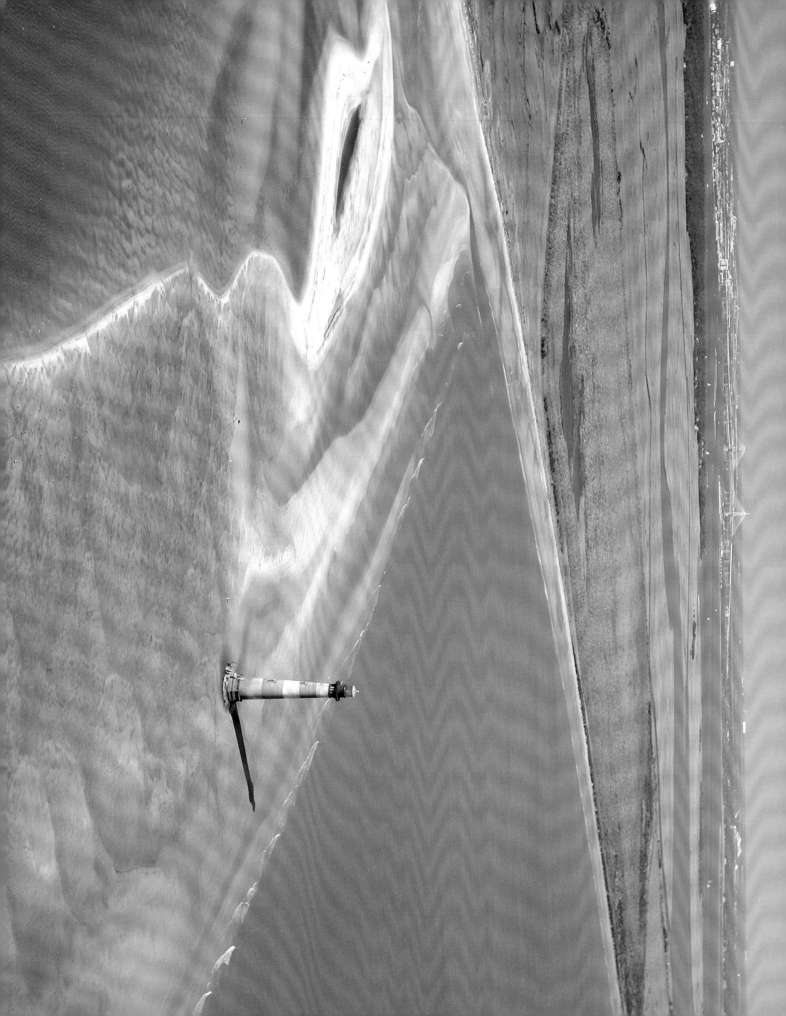

Opposite: Aerial view of Morris Island Lighthouse

Aerial view of Sullivan's Island Lighthouse

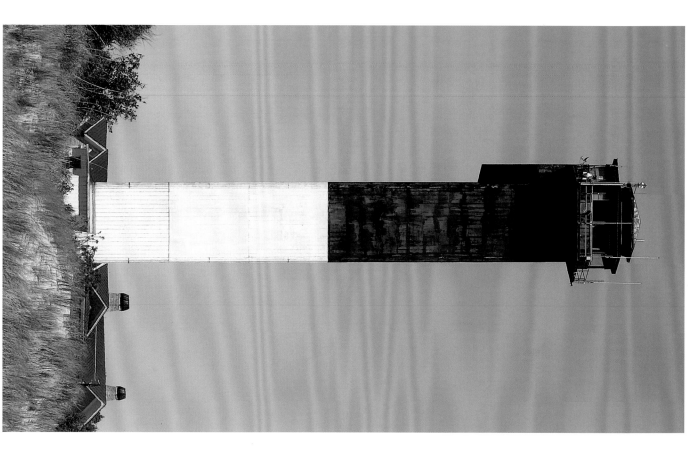

Sullivan's Island Lighthouse

The U.S. Coast Guard took over control of American lighthouses in 1939, and soon decided that the encroaching ocean would doom the Morris Island tower. By the time the old light was decommissioned in 1962, it was surrounded by water at high tide, as it is today.

Back near the spot where 17th-century fires showed ships the way, the Sullivan's Island lighthouse went into service in 1962, and the 20th-century marvel is literally an example of how far the lighthouse mystique could go. Anchored by steel girders on a concrete foundation, the 163-foot tower was built of aluminum paneling in a triangular pattern to withstand the most severe hurricanes. Its original candlepower capacity was so intense that it was feared the lighthouse could temporarily blind mariners, and was reduced to 1,170,000 candlepower in 1967 - still strong enough to be seen far beyond the limits of American territorial waters.

Although Sullivan's Island would boast the first American lighthouse to feature an elevator and air-conditioning, the beacon could not stem a turning tide of global positioning technology that reduced the need for visual references, and would be the last of its kind built in the United States. Fully automated in 1982, the light on Sullivan's Island is still in service, but has joined its predecessor across the harbor channel on Morris Island in a greatly reduced role.

Of course, being in Charleston, relics have a way of hanging on, as has the Morris Island light. Nearly fifty years after it was in use, and pounded daily by waves, wind and old age, the great old tower still stands strong and somewhat straight in defiance of all the odds against it.

Having been such a visible part of the sea and landscape for so many generations, the Morris Island light has glimmered as the focus of nostalgia, and in 2000 was leased to a group known as Save the Light, Inc., for 99 years.

Hopes are to raise enough money to build a cofferdam base to secure the light against the sea, and allow this historic area to keep intact another shining beacon of a glorious past.

CHARLESTONESE

or many years, Charlestonians have shared the singular experience of being asked for directions by tourists, who, after listening for a few seconds, excused themselves politely by saying, "Oh, we're sorry, we thought you spoke English." Those visitors should have known, of course, that true Charlestonians only speak English occasionally, and even when doing so, habitually use terms that are never found in Webster's Dictionary.

The peculiar vernacular known as "Charlestonese" comes from a variety of diverse dialects that have simmered for centuries in the same melting pot - a colorful mix of accents, syntax and vocabulary whose roots range from the Scottish highlands to the plains of West Africa . From this lingual fusion came audible confusion that would confound telephone operators for years to come, and despite the influx of accentless disc jockeys and monotoned television anchors, is still a way of speaking easily distinguishable from any other region in America.

Charlestonians are often mistaken as British or Canadians because of their "oo" pronunciation of the vowel combination "ou". Many a visitor has been dumbfounded when invited into a "hoos" (house), or has looked down at their shoes when hearing "a boot" (about). Of course, the original Charlestonians were from the British Isles, but somewhere along the line they dropped English accents along with some "r's", while picking up a local flavor as well as a few "y's".

In Charlestonese tradition, "car" is pronounced "cyah", "garment" is "gyahment", and "girl" becomes "gyuhl". Such twists in sound may explain the trouble one stranded Charlestonian driver had after telling a northern highway patrolman that he tried to "shoot"(shout) at people to help get his "cyar stahted"(car started).

Local lingo was so heavily-laced with the Scots-Irish brogue of colonial immigrants that today, Charlestonians are better understood in Edinburgh than in New York City, which, come to think of it, may not be such a bad thing. The Celtic flavor is readily-evident as "to" is pronounced "toe", "day" is "deh", "wish" becomes "wush", and "pot" is "pawt". But the tongue-twisters don't stop there, as "late" becomes "leyet", "smile" is "smoil", and "taste" sounds like "teys".

Some consonants have been mouthed less on Charleston lips than unpeeled shrimp, resulting in such pronunciations as "poach" for "porch", "fowit" for "fort", "rychuh" for "right here" and "doze" for "those". A local hunter once pointed out some deer to his out-of-town companion while explaining that females of the species were strictly off limits, saying in perfect Charlestonese, "doze deh uh does, doe"(those there are does, though).

Another major local influence comes from a dialect used by descendants of West Africans known as Gullah. Retaining some genuine terms from places like Sierra Leone and Gabon such as "cootuh"(turtle), "yam"(sweet potato) and "gumbo"(soup), Gullah is laced with contorted combinations of English grammar as well, so that "on top of" becomes "pontop", "both of those" is "all too dem", "to catch" becomes "fuh ketchum", and "going to" translates as "gwine dee".

One distinctive characteristic of Gullah is its colorful assortment of physically-descriptive metaphors. Thus "ee fut in ee han" literally means "his foot is in his hand", referring to the image of a running rabbit, stretching back legs forward over its front legs, and translates simply to " he's fast", while someone who smiles does, in Gullah terms, "crack ee teet" or "crack his teeth".

Naturally, Charlestonians like to save their most baffling linguistics for tourists. Anyone who speaks Charlestonese is called a "binyuh"(been here), and is easily distinguished from the twangs and drawls of a visiting "cumyuh"(come here), and it can be great sport to make oneself deliberately harder to understand when asked a question.

Imagine the plight of the New Englander who requested directions to an address on South Battery, hearing, "Oid goo sreyet pas dee stawp soin en teyek dee lef dountoedee gyahdin geyet widee gowul leyuf, dass noinee-noin". It was Charlestonese for, "I'd go straight past the stop sign and take the left down to the garden gate with the gold leaf, that's ninety-nine".

Or consider the lunching Midwesterner who had the misfortune to ask for recommendations from a local waitress. "Moi fehvrut is troot fulleh wut mulk 'n cole shrump," she said, lapsing into Charlestonese, "butchoo cehyint biyet dee hawt pleyet 'n buscuts wit greveh, jis meyek shoe yoe leeiv sum rum foe disut". Translation - "my favorite is the trout fillet with milk and cold shrimp, but you can't beat the hot plate and biscuits with gravy, just make sure you leave some room for dessert."

But the classic in audible exasperation was the example given by the late Charleston story-teller Dick Reeves about the New York hunter who, when unable to get a shot from his position on a deer stand, asked his Gullah-speaking guide to change places. "Nosah," he was told, "wen onuh deh de deh de no de deh, buonuh aindeh de deh de deh deh", a Gullah version of Murphy's Law meaning, "No, when you're there, the deer is never there, but when you're not there the deer is there".

With time, the uniqueness of local speech has faded, and some multi-generational Charlestonians are now actually fluent in every-day English. But there's still genuine Charlestonese spoken here an there, and an easy way to find it is by simply asking any one who claims to be versed in it how to say certain words. True Charlestonians will pronounce "Moultrie" as "Mootree", "Legare" as "Lugree", "Vanderhorst" as "Vandross", "Edisto" as "Edeestoe", and say "Cooper" as if the vowels rhyme with "cooker". If the speaker says these words in any other fashion, walk away - it's just another "cumyuh".

The Charm of

CHARLESTON

ARCHITECTURE, CULTURE, AND NATURE

Stories of The South Carolina Lowcountry